God, give me entrance [into the] hearts of the lost, without them knowing it. Holy Spirit, bring life + Your purpose to all I do. Make me Your instrument - effective + inspiring that ppl will be won by your Spirit + bond slaves to my / the world's Saviour, Jesus the Christ

MISSING PIECES

real hope when
life doesn't make sense

What is God saying to me now? As we walk c the Lord, He will speak varying things, according to His word, in different seasons.

JENNIFER ROTHSCHILD

LifeWay Press®
Nashville, Tennessee

Published by LifeWay Press®
© 2012 • Jennifer Rothschild

Reprinted July 2020

ISBN 978-1-4158-6997-0
Item 005371621

Dewey decimal classification: 234.2
Subject headings: FAITH \ GOD \ CHRISTIAN LIFE

To order additional copies of this resource, write to LifeWay Church Resources Customer Service; One LifeWay Plaza; Nashville, TN 37234-0113; fax 615.251.5933; phone 800.458.2772; email orderentry@lifeway.com; or order online at www.lifeway.com.

Printed in the United States of America

Adult Publishing
LifeWay Church Resources
One LifeWay Plaza
Nashville, TN 37234-0152

contents

About the Author

Missing Pieces: Real Hope When Life Doesn't Make Sense is Jennifer's fourth video-based Bible study with LifeWay. It follows her popular Bible study, *Me, Myself, and Lies: A Thought-Closet Makeover.*

Jennifer has been cleaning out her thought closet and reconciling the missing pieces in her blanket of faith ever since her life drastically changed at the age of 15 when she lost her sight. Now, more than 30 years later, she boldly and compassionately teaches women how to walk by faith, not by sight.

Known for her substance, signature wit, and down-to-earth style, Jennifer weaves together colorful illustrations, Biblical principles, and music to help women live empowered. As a speaker, author, and accomplished singer-songwriter she travels internationally, offering fresh, sensible, biblical advice to audiences who, like her, are determined to pursue healthy and fulfilling lives in spite of their circumstances. She has shared her practical and inspiring messages to arena-sized audiences across the country and media outlets including *Dr. Phil, Good Morning America, Life Today,* The Learning Channel, and *The Billy Graham Television Special.*

Jennifer is an avid listener of audio books, is a C.S. Lewis junkie, and has a weakness for dark chocolate and robust coffee. She and her Dr. Phil live in Springfield, Missouri, and have two sons, Connor and Clayton, and a lovely daughter-in-law, Caroline. When she is not traveling, Jennifer enjoys nature walks and riding a bicycle built for two.

Jennifer is also the featured teacher and founder of Fresh Grounded Faith Conferences and publisher of the popular online magazine for women in ministry called *womensministry.net.*

Introduction

Some things just don't make sense, why do men's hair lines get higher while women's bust lines get lower? But far more significant—if God is good, why do we suffer? Why are children treated unjustly? Why doesn't God heal when He is capable? When the hard stuff becomes personal, our questions become piercing.

- A spouse leaves … God, do You care?
- You see injustice in the world … God, is this fair?
- You wonder if you will ever stop feeling lonely because you long for a baby, a spouse, a friend … God, are You there?
- You get a pink slip instead of a paycheck … God, are You aware?
- You ask God for years to help you lose weight, be more patient, overcome your temper … God, do You hear my prayer?
- Nothing in your life seems to make sense and you just feel like you could have your own book of the Bible, kinda like Job … God, do You err?

Because I became blind as a teenager, I've asked all these questions. They have the potential to create "missing pieces" in our faith. We aren't the only ones with missing pieces though. For thousands of years, both the faithful and faithless have had questions. In the seventh-century B.C., Habakkuk was a prophet. The people of Judah were doing evil things and Habakkuk asked God, "How long, Lord, must I call for help and You do not listen? … Why do You force me to look at injustice?" (1:2-3). God responded that Judah was to be attacked by the Chaldeans (see v. 6). Habakkuk's people were about to suffer greatly, and he just didn't understand. His questions had to create missing pieces in his faith.

Habakkuk had a response that's hard for me to understand. In chapter 3 he said, "Though the fig tree does not bud and there is no fruit on the vines, though the olive crop fails and the fields produce no food, though there are no sheep in the pen and no cattle in the stalls, yet I will triumph in Yahweh; I will rejoice in the God of my salvation!" (vv. 17-18). Habakkuk knew the olive crops would fail and

figs wouldn't blossom. He knew the fields would be barren with no cattle. The only thing he could count on was heartache and loss—missing pieces. But, his response was rejoicing? Wow!

Do you know why he could be content enough to rejoice, even in such loss? It was because his satisfaction didn't come from answers. Habakkuk's satisfaction and hope came from the encounter with God his questions caused. Unanswered questions can be the missing pieces that help us really know God. That's what we really want, isn't it? To know God intimately, not just know about Him.

As you begin this study, I want you to think about your favorite blanket. You know, the one that keeps you warm a cold winter day. The one you wrap up in to watch a movie. Maybe it's the one you've had since you were a girl. My guess is it might be a little worn; maybe a bit tattered or frayed. Your blanket might even have some missing pieces.

Now think about how your faith is like that blanket. It provides you comfort and security, yet it can also be tattered and frayed by the questions that emerge from heartache and trials you have endured. Each sorrow we face can create a hole in our faith, a missing piece.

I want you to wrap yourself in that blanket as you begin each day in our time together. I'm going to call it your blanket of faith. Feel how it warms and protects you. That is what your faith, holes and all, does for you.

During this study, you may experience lots of different feelings. Feelings like discouragement, disappointment, or anger seem to always show up with our missing pieces. I want you to come visit me at *JenniferRothschild.com/MP* weekly (or as often as you'd like). I want to answer your questions, respond to your comments and provide you some additional helpful resources. In fact, each week I have a different "freebie" for you to enjoy as well as downloads, bonus videos from me, and some practical resources I've collected.

We are on this journey together so let's trust in the Lord with all our hearts, not lean on what we understand, but in all our ways let's acknowledge Him and see how He directs our paths. I pray that God will fill your missing pieces with Himself.

Jennifer

Get a free download or CD of Jennifer's song "Take Me to the Cross," featured in *Missing Pieces*, by visiting *JenniferRothschild.com/MP*

Group Session  1

Video Notes

God does _____,_____, and
_____ our questions.

When we're _____ _____
we wonder where God is.

God wants to fill the missing pieces with _____.

We don't want to just know _____ God. We want to
_____ God.

Conversation Guide

1. Consider a "low point" that made you want to give up. What, if anything, prevented you from taking your hard questions to the Lord in that situation?

2. How might humbly presenting your questions to God illustrate your faith in Him?

3. Identify holes in your own blanket of faith. What about the analogy most resonates with you?

DOWNLOADS

· ·

Video and audio sessions are available at *lifeway.com/jenniferrothschild*

Get a free download or CD of Jennifer's song "Take Me to the Cross" at *JenniferRothschild.com/MP*

week one

God, Do You Care?

In the wilderness of sorrow we all sometimes wonder if God cares. *If God is a God of compassion, why doesn't He just deliver me?* Caught in this missing piece, we can feel miserable.

The Israelites could relate. They were a miserable group, surrounded by God's care and compassion that fell every morning in the form of manna. Though they knew God cared, they remained unhappy; that's why I call them the Miserable-ites! "Who will feed us meat? We remember the free fish we ate in Egypt, along with the cucumbers, melons, leeks, onions, and garlic. But now our appetite is gone; there's nothing to look at but this manna!" (Num. 11:4-6). They whined as if to say, "God, all we get is what You provided."

Rescued from Egypt, daily provided for, why were they so miserable? Surrounded by God's provision, they were miserable because they didn't receive it. They may have eaten, but they didn't take it in, acknowledge it for what it was—God's kindness, grace. They were consumed with misery, bitterness, and hopelessness. They thought if God cared, He would provide onions and melons. They missed the grace that fell each day with the dew because they took it for granted and didn't recognize it as God's compassion and grace.

We too can think God doesn't care because we miss His provision. We become consumed with our own lack. We don't notice His compassion and faithfulness. To experience God's care, we must receive His compassion in whatever portion and form He chooses to express it.

He wants to give you His manna as a reminder of His grace and compassion. To receive it, we need to have an open hand and heart. Only open hands receive. You cannot receive with a clenched fist. God cares. Let go of whatever is in your hands, open them to God and receive.

Day 1 If God Cares, Why Won't He Act?

I discovered a laundry defect gene. I decided it must exist when I stumbled upon a lump of dirty clothes strewn before my 12-year-old son's laundry basket. I've marveled for years how my PhD husband Phil can't seem to put his laundry in the hamper—he drops it in front of the basket. He's capable of placing it inside, he just doesn't. It's a mystery. Reconciled to my husband's quirky behavior, I've moved on. That is, until the day I literally stumbled on my son Connor's mound of manhood. "What is this?" I yelled from his bathroom. Connor ran expecting to find an insect or leak in the ceiling. My tone did sound a little shocked and urgent. "What Mom? Are you OK?"

"Laundry in front of the basket? Are you serious? Why isn't it in the basket?"

"I don't know Mom."

I peppered him with questions like, "Are you able to put it in?" After he said yes, I asked, "Why don't you put it in then?" He was as perplexed as I was, so I just determined it must be genetic. I'm doomed to empty baskets and mounds of laundry in front of them for all my days I guess!

Because Connor is able to do something but chooses not to, it's more frustrating than if he were unable to do something and therefore did not do it. The same applies to God. If He is able to do something in our lives—like heal or deliver—but doesn't act, it can be frustrating and cause more questions than answers.

Do you ever feel frustrated when you consider your own circumstances? I mean, if God can do something, like heal or rescue, why doesn't He? Underline any of the thoughts you've had.

- I must have weak faith or this wouldn't be happening.
- Maybe I am not praying hard enough or correctly.
- Perhaps God is too busy to notice.
- My problems don't matter. God only cares about the big things like earthquakes and wars.
- God must be mad at me because of sin in my life.

You may have underlined more than one of the thoughts and that's OK. We will deal with lots of questions over the coming weeks but ponder what you underlined and think about why you chose what you did. Let's just consider one of those options together: Does God care? If He lets trying circumstances continue when He could fix it, is it because He just doesn't care?

What does Job 10:12 say about God's care for us?

How does Psalm 103:13 describe God?

What adjectives does Jonah 4:2 use to describe God's character?

God has a caring character which preserves us, and His nature is that of a good Father. He's compassionate and, yet, sometimes His care feels as if He is MIA.

Have you ever felt a lack of compassion from God? If so, describe.

How do you feel He should have reacted to your situation?

Why do you think God doesn't always show His compassion in an obvious way?

What does the psalmist ask in Psalm 77:8-9?

The psalmist was dealing with some missing pieces, and he wondered if God's lovingkindness ceased and if His promise came to an end. David was so tangled in his own pain that he questioned if God simply got angry and stopped being compassionate or maybe He just forgot to be caring. If you've felt that way or feel that way right now, Sister, you're in good company. Pain makes us wonder if God has forgotten to care about us.

What does Isaiah 49:15 say about God's compassion toward you and God remembering you?

A mother cannot possibly forget her child whether that baby is 21 days old or 21 years old. If you're not a mom, you still understand intuitively that urge to love and nurture. It's how women are wired, and that's why Isaiah uses such imagery about God. Moms don't forget, and neither does God.

When our oldest son Clayton had emergency surgery as an 8-month-old baby it was such a difficult day for us. I was nursing at the time and had to stop immediately. And, if you've nursed a baby before, you know that's not the most ideal way to stop! It's extremely painful. Let me just say this Sister; even if I wanted to forget my baby and forget being compassionate, I could not. My personal pain kept my son's pain front and center. I chose not to forget and I could not forget.

If I as a feeble, human mom have that within me, how much more does your Heavenly Father remember you and desire to show you His compassion? If you didn't have a mom that showed you compassion, please know she did not reflect the heart of God. Her weakness misrepresented who God is.

God doesn't forget to be compassionate, but sometimes His compassion is obscure and hard to recognize.

When you consider your difficult trials, it may be hard to understand how God can truly care if He lets it remain. Why doesn't He show His compassion in a way we'd recognize? Or maybe a better question is "Why does He show His compassion in such a mysterious way?" Think about that. Could God be showing His compassion by allowing your pain to remain rather than by removing it? How could your pain or unanswered questions represent God's care for you? Ask yourself the following questions.

Has my pain been a source of protection for me? If so, how?

Has my pain taught me something about God or myself? If so, what?

Has my pain put me in a position I may not have been without it?
If so, where?

After you ask yourself those questions, call one of your Bible study buddies and share with her your insights. Your honesty will encourage her and strengthen you.

We often assume God's apparent inactivity in our situation is evidence of His neglect, when it really may be His way of showing compassion to protect you, provide for you, or preserve you.

Pray and ask God to affirm His care for you and show you how afflictions and pain can be evidence of His compassion.

A piece of comfort from George MacDonald:

"Afflictions are but the shadows of God's wings."[1]

Day 2 Do You Not Care?

Well, I hope you don't get seasick because today we're heading out to the Sea of Galilee! The story in Mark 4 will help answer the question of God's care for us.

> Who initiated the crossing of the Sea of Galilee in Mark 4:35—the disciples or Jesus?

> Do you think Jesus knew a storm would erupt while they were on their voyage?

> If Jesus knew there would be a storm, why do you think He would send them into such a scary, dangerous situation?

The NIV wording of verse 36 reports the condition of Christ when they entered the boat as, "Just as he was." Mark was probably referring to Jesus' status at the time; they took Him with them just as He was. In other words, He didn't change clothes or grab a sandwich before boarding the vessel. But, think of that phrase in a broader sense: God is compassionate. Do you take Him "just as He is"? Do you take God for who He is, even if He expresses His care in a confusing way?

> Have you ever tried to change God into what you want Him to be like?

> Circle the image that best depicts what or who you expect God to be in your life.
>
> | servant | boss | magic genie |
> |---|---|---|
> | best friend | father | other: |

Often we feel real disappointment with God because we are unwilling to take Him just as He is. Until we do, we will be frustrated with our faith.

> How have you felt disappointed with God just as He is?

Back to the boat …

In verse 37, Mark tells us a storm erupted when they were well into their journey.

> Underline the statement below which best depicts what verse 38 says Christ was doing during the storm.
> 1. standing in front, bailing out water
> 2. grasping the rails, praying to God the Father
> 3. hugging scared disciples, comforting them with His words
> 4. lying in the stern, asleep on the cushion
> 5. calming the storm

Jesus was asleep! When a storm rages, we don't like to think of our God as sleeping through it.

> If you were in the boat, which of the above positions would you have preferred Jesus to be in?

We sometimes want to picture Jesus bailing out water, praying to God, hugging His followers, or fixing the problem altogether—doing something would make us feel like He cared. But, He slept. Are we willing to take Him just as He is? The disciples weren't.

> They woke Him saying what (v. 38)?

His frightened followers did not ask, "Do You care?" Instead, they asked, "Do You not care?" To ask Jesus, "Do You care?" is to inquire. But, to ask, "Don't You care?" is an accusation hidden in the form of a question. Hear the difference?

> The words below describe the actions of inquirers and of accusers. Place an *A* by words that describe the actions of an accuser and an *I* beside the words that befit the actions of an inquirer.
>
> ___ seek   ___ wonder   ___ request
>
> ___ judge   ___ condemn   ___ assume
>
> ___ ask   ___ criticize

> Can you identify? If someone accuses you in the form of a question, how does it feel?

Do you tend to inquire of God or to accuse Him? Which of the word(s) in the last activity best describes the way you approach God when you are mired in pain or caught in a storm? Circle the word from the list.

Do you believe those words are the best way to approach God? Do they show you are taking God as He is? Why or why not?

If you need to, stop right now and pray about this. You may want to call a friend to process this. Remember, God loves you. He offers no condemnation when we are struggling. He does, however, expect His children to talk to Him about it.

The disciples asked Jesus their question, but the unspoken accusation was "He obviously doesn't care about frightened followers!" They then followed their accusatory question with an assumption.

What did they assume? (See v. 38b.) "… that we're _____"

✳ **Note:** Accusers usually have an agenda. They usually are operating on assumptions. Inquirers are open to answers—even answers they don't like.

Which one are you most often?

"Don't You care that we're going to die?" They asked the question with the assumption that they were going to die, and the assumption was faulty because it was speculative. Do you do that? The disciples didn't know they would die in the storm. They thought or felt they'd die in the storm.

When you ask God questions, do you base it on assumption or speculation? "Don't You care my marriage is rocky, we'll divorce, and I'll end up alone and miserable?" "Don't You care my teenager is hanging out with the wrong kids and will become a drug addict and ruin his life?" "Don't You care that my illness might leave my kids without a mother?"

Write your own exaggerated statement below which relates to your situation and let it end with speculation.

"Don't You care that …

Now, think about that speculative possible outcome. When you're losing hope or when the storm is tossing you, remember what you wrote is speculation and, thus, a faulty assumption. Don't let your fear take you there. Instead, take God as He is and trust that He cares because He is in the boat with you.

What we know, what we think, and what we feel are not always the best representation of reality.

You may know your marriage is rocky or your teen is hanging out with the wrong crowd, but that doesn't mean the worst possible outcome is inevitable. Storms do not equal death. Don't fall into the pit of despair by jumping on the slippery slide of assuming the worst.

You cannot control storms, but you can control your assumptions. When the wind was raging and the boat was being tossed, to the disciples death was a possible outcome, but it was not the only possible outcome.

Sometimes our speculation is based solely on our feelings—like fear, insecurity, and hopelessness.

If the disciples' assumption of certain death was not based on fact and truth, perhaps their assumption that Jesus didn't care was also an incorrect representation of Christ. Is that possible?

We can't assess storms based on our assumptions or speculations nor can we assess God based on our assumptions or speculations either.

As you face your own pain and questions, you may think you will die; you may feel you won't make it. "I feel" and "I think" thoughts are often based on speculation and assumption. God is not "I feel," He is "I Am" (see Ex. 3:14).

For you and me to become who we long to be we must take God as He is.

In Mark 4:39, Jesus spoke peace. Read that verse aloud.

How beautiful that Jesus didn't first rebuke His disciples; He rebuked the storm and He spoke peace.

My friend, the God who cares is in your boat. The peace He grants is not reserved for storms; it is intended for your heart.

Don't let the fact that God allows a storm in your life, and you can't understand why, cause you to isolate yourself from the God you need most.

If you really think God is sleeping through your storm, then grab your blanket of faith and go snuggle up right there with Him. As you rest in Him you will find the peace you long for and realize how deeply Father God cares for you.

A piece of my mind:
God is not "I feel" or "I think." God is "I Am."

Day 3 Compassionate Inactivity

By now you've had time to grapple with what it means to take God at His Word and trust that He cares. Even if you're willing to believe He does care, you may still be left with the problem of His inactivity when you consider the suffering that doesn't seem to make sense. Questions still remain. Does He avoid stepping in and cleaning things up because He can't? Did He set the world in motion but then abdicate His power to someone else so He is bound to inaction? Maybe He does care, but He doesn't have the ability to intervene. Hmm …

What does Jeremiah 18:1-6 suggest about God's power?

God can do what He chooses with His people. He has the power and ability to create and recreate, shape and destroy. God shows His power "as it pleased the potter" (v. 4, NASB). In other words, God shows His power in the way He chooses. And, it isn't always as we choose, is it?

God's power is beyond our ability to perceive or grasp. He is omnipotent. That literally means all-powerful. Since God is powerful beyond bounds, why doesn't He act when we ask? Consider the following story in formulating your answer.

When my husband Phil and I were newlyweds, we lived in a rackety shackety little apartment in West Palm Beach, Florida. We were smack-dab in the middle of the worst part of town and had our bikes and grill stolen to prove it! Blaring sirens serenaded us each night as we fell asleep. I wasn't fond of this less-than-secure environment, but Phil found it a stage upon which he could perform his heroics. On several occasions he chased away "bad guys" from our backyard, once when he was wearing a shabby pair of torn gym shorts. It was bad enough that the criminal and police saw him dressed that way, but unfortunately, the vice president of the university where Phil taught came upon the crime scene just in time to behold my shirtless husband in all his saggy gym shorts splendor.

The story Phil most loves from his super hero days in Crimeville was the time he saw a guy dart behind our apartment carrying a TV. Faster than a speeding bullet (well, you know) Phil ran outside and began to chase the bad guy. (This time fully dressed I might add.) Bad guy saw Phil. Bad guy dropped TV. Phil trailed him for blocks until the hooligan got into a congested part of town. At that point, the bad guy began to walk casually along the sidewalk blending into the crowd. Phil was concerned the bad guy may have a gun so he hid behind trees and followed him covertly while the bad guy tried to hide among pedestrians. The police had been called and their sirens alerted my husband that help was on the way. As soon as the patrol car pulled up, Phil jumped from behind a bush and ran toward the villain; he threw himself at his ankles, hooked them in his arm, and yelled "Officer, I got him for you!" It was a proud and powerful Barney Fife moment!

My husband's antics showed off his power but highlighted the fact that he lacked authority. Power without authority isn't complete. He could have clung to the bad guy's ankles for hours if he was strong and powerful enough, but he never could have accomplished any justice because he lacked authority.

Authority trumps power every time. God possesses both ultimate power and ultimate authority. The choice to not exercise power does not mean one is powerless. It means sometimes one who has power chooses to withhold it for a greater purpose.

Healing, delivering, and calming a troubled sea all show God has power over people and creation. But a greater evidence of His power and care is His exercise of power over Himself.

> **What does Romans 9:22-23 suggest about God's apparent suspension of power? Why doesn't He show His power?**

God endured our sinfulness with patience. He did this to make known the riches of His mercies and forbearance.

> **What does that mean to you?**

Our sin deserves God's wrath. The fact that God chooses to forbear instead of destroy reveals a power and compassion you and I can't even comprehend. To understand the power He possesses, it's important to understand the nature of "the riches of his … forbearance" (Rom. 2:4, ESV). Some versions render this word as kindness, tolerance, or patience. The Greek word, *anoche*, or *forbearance*, is best understood as a picture.[2] Visualize the hand of God, lifted, ready to strike a just blow against the sinner. Just then, the other hand of God rises to stop the strike by grasping the arm and pulling it back. In His restraint He displays He has power over Himself. This compassion for us is far more magnificent than displaying power over created elements. He chooses not to act even though He could. He chooses to forbear.

What reason for God's apparent inactivity does Hosea 5:15 suggest?

God sometimes chooses not to act out of compassion. He does so to give us time to acknowledge our sin or seek Him.

How does that apply to your painful or confusing circumstances? Does your hard situation let you or someone else see your need for Him? Can you see God's purpose? Jot down your thoughts.

What does Isaiah 30:18 tell you is another reason for God's restraint?

God's restraint and forbearance show His compassion for the purpose of drawing you to Himself. Oh, my friend, I know you're trying to trust Him and understand His ways. I struggle with the same. I'm fully confident God cares about me and could heal my blindness, but even though He has the power to, He doesn't choose to show it in the way I sometimes hope—not yet anyway. Does that mean He doesn't care? I think it means He cares enough to allow me to struggle and find a deeper understanding of and connection to His heart.

If I plead for His power, then I must accept His authority that comes along with it. Stop for a second and think about that statement. I'll say it again—this time to you directly. If you plead for His power, then you must accept His authority that comes along with it. His power may be capable of healing my eyes and filling in your missing pieces, but His authority may not deem it best. I'm learning to respectfully trust His authority as much as I trust His power. For it is the companionship of those two attributes that allows suffering and at the same time disallows punishment for our sin. Hard truths, I know. But, unless we take God just as He is in His wholeness, we will never find hope in our own brokenness.

So, should God heal you just because He can? Should God end that trial to ease your faith questions? Should He deliver you just because He is able to? Should God hold you accountable for your sin just because He has the right to? Consider this with me: To embrace the concept of forbearance as it applies to our sins, yet, reject it as it applies to our suffering, is to reject part of the character of God. And if we don't experience His wholeness, we will never experience our own.

PRAYER FOR TODAY

God grant me understanding and grace to plead for Your power and at the same time accept Your authority. Help me to forbear during my difficulties as You forbear patiently my sin. May I take You as You are. Amen.

Day 4 Special Delivery with Care

News flash! Blindness makes me tired! My friend Karen once told me that I make blindness look easy. I laughed because it isn't easy at all. Yet, she said that because people only see the "polished" result of all the raw refining that comes with blindness. I share this with you because I want you to know I get it— I understand how trials and hard stuff can make us frustrated and feel defeated. Sometimes our fatigue is greater than our faith. It takes perseverance to keep wrestling with the missing pieces.

Sometimes, we want our powerful, caring Father God to deliver us from our pain. We can wonder, *since He is powerful and caring, why won't the Deliverer deliver?* Or maybe a better question is, *why does the Deliverer do His delivering in such a mysterious way?*

Pour yourself a cup of coffee or tea. Today let's just talk honestly as sisters. I want to share with you a hard story about God's care and deliverance.

It was 1983, and I was on a college choir tour with First Baptist Church West Palm Beach. Shari and I had been sharing a room on tour, and we were also sharing clothes and secrets. Lots of us girls at Palm Beach Atlantic College and FBC were close, and that's why our tour was abruptly interrupted and completely deflated when we got the news about our friend Regina. Regina didn't come with us that year on tour. She went home when spring semester ended. She was a vivacious redhead who truly always smiled. Of course, I couldn't see her smile but I could hear it and I could feel it. She was warm and kind and it was so clear that she really loved God. Our director waited until after our concert to tell us what happened to Regina. She had been riding her bike—as she always did—in a park near her home. She was attacked, raped, and strangled. She was left unclothed in some brush in the park. This was our dear, sweet friend. It wasn't a character on a TV crime show—it was Regina. We were all shaken and disheartened.

If this could happen to Regina, then does God really care about anyone? She loved Him. Why didn't He deliver her? On the bus after the concert, those were the questions intertwined with the tears.

Our tour ended too late for us to attend her funeral. When I got home, I sat in the living room with my dad. I couldn't hold back tears as I retold what Regina endured. I kept asking him, "How could God let her go through that?"

Have you ever asked that question about your or someone else's painful circumstance? What circumstance prompted the question?

That's so hard, isn't it? After all, God promises to deliver us and clearly, He didn't. At least that's how I felt.

In Dad's attempt to console me, he quietly spoke in his gentle southern drawl. "She didn't go through it." His statement startled me. "She went from it." He explained how God sometimes protects us from awful things so we never have to endure them. That's a form of His deliverance. Sometimes, God delivers us by rescuing or healing us. Sometimes, God brings us successfully through hard things—that's also a form of His deliverance. But, sometimes out of His great care for His children, He delivers us out of the horror and into His glory.

Unlike us, who, if we lived through such agony, would have a marred and awful memory, God compassionately took Regina out of that situation and into His presence. She was brought from it, out of it, and into glory where no tears, no crying, and no pain exist. The only scars are the ones on the hands of Jesus. I now think of Regina as she should be remembered. She is not a victim; she is a victor. The question remains: Did God really deliver her as He promises?

Fill in the rest of the stories below to see how God delivers us.

2 Kings 6:15-20—God delivered Elisha and the Israelites ...

Isaiah 38:1-5—God delivered Hezekiah ...

Daniel 3:16-28—God delivered the three young Hebrew men ...

Acts 6:8-15; 7:54-60—God delivered Stephen ...

Based on what the Bible describes as God's deliverance, I believe God delivered Regina. It wasn't in the way I would have chosen, yet I believe it was His compassionate choice.

My friend, you may have endured something so awful that you are weeping right now just recalling it and wondering why God let you go through it. The fact that you are doing this study tells me you are gutsy and willing to push yourself even through your fear, frustration, or fatigue. What has been such a huge missing piece in your life can become a place others will deposit their tears and find hope even when their lives don't make sense. God does care. I care. Your Bible study buddies care. Keep holding on.

> **Matthew 4:1 describes another type of deliverance that is really, really tough. To where was Jesus delivered? Who led Him and why?**
>
> The _____ led Jesus into the _____ to be
> _____.

Sometimes God wills to lead us into hardship just as Jesus was led by the Spirit into the wilderness. Perhaps the wilderness wanderings of the Hebrew people give us a hint why God sometimes delivers us into our own places of wilderness.

> **What does Deuteronomy 8:2-3 suggest as the purposes of being led into the wilderness?**

God allowed His children to roam the wilderness for 40 years to humble them, test them, expose what was in their hearts, and determine whether or not they would keep and depend on God's Word.

> **Think about the mystery of faith you deal with in your situation. As you consider it, circle one of the Israelite's deliverance lessons from bottom of page 24 that describes what you may be learning from your trial. Has the Master Potter used it to humble you, test you, or draw you to His Word?**

After you circle one (or more) write a "Thank You, Lord" note for what you are learning.

Dear God,

Amen

Check the kind of deliverance you think of when you think about your own situation.

○ God is delivering me through hardship like He did the three Hebrew young men in the fiery furnace.
○ God is/has/will deliver me from hardship through healing or rescue like He did for Hezekiah.
○ God has delivered me by preventing hardship like He did for the Israelites and Elisha.
○ God has delivered me into hardship like His Spirit led Jesus to be tempted.

Each of the stories about God's deliverance features a positive faith statement.

Write each one beside the appropriate person, but personalize it as an "I" statement and make it your own. I'll start with the first one.

Hezekiah; Isaiah 38:17
I am rescued from destruction because of God's love for me.

Hebrew young men; Daniel 3:17-18

_____

Elisha; 2 Kings 6:16

_____

Jesus; Matthew 4:4

_____

Choose the statement of faith you most need to claim in your hard moments. Rephrase it and write it in all caps here as if you're screaming it out with all your heart.

When you get sucked into the deep hole of despair, let your statement of faith be a way God delivers you from it. Speak it to yourself and pray it to your Father. Write it on a card or in lipstick on your bathroom mirror.

However God chooses to deliver us really is a reflection of His compassion. Delivering us into hard stuff, through hard stuff, and from hard stuff all show God's compassion and care. "You placed burdens on our backs. ... But You brought us out to abundance" (Ps. 66:11-12).

A piece of truth from one who knows:
"You gave me life and faithful love, and Your care has guarded my life." *Job 10:12*

Day 5 The God of Empathy

Maybe this will be the year she smiles, I thought while waiting for my annual physical. The doctor I had seen for the last many years was a good doctor, but she sorely lacked in bedside manners—and manners in general. She entered my room and by the dull, monotone sound of her voice, I realized this wasn't the year for her smile. She droned through her usual questions about new meds and commenting on weight, blood pressure, and such. *She still hasn't looked up at me,* I thought. I knew she hadn't because her voice was droning into her clipboard. Then, the exam began. She's a fine doctor, but I've had better interactions with empty cardboard boxes. (And they're much cheaper.)

She finished and asked, "Do you have any questions?" with that tone that suggests "you better not" and then shot out of the room before I could answer.

As I dressed, *I thought I'm 47; a big girl! If I don't want to use this doc anymore, I don't have to. This is my last time!* I felt empowered as I passed the receptionist without an appointment for the following year. The next year arrived, and it was time for a new doctor. I found a general physician, and when she entered my examination room, she was effusive and warm. *I like her,* I thought. *She's more interesting than a cardboard box.* She asked questions. Her voice never fell flatly on the ground and was not once swallowed by a clipboard. She was actually making eye contact. She listened and took her time, and even the room didn't feel so frigid. Then, she told me we were the same age and many of the changes I was experiencing, she was too.

When I told her I felt fuzzy headed and moodier more than I used too, she laughed and said she could identify. "There's something that can help with your memory and moods," she said. "It's called … uh, um … it's called … uh, um … It's a memory-enhancing supplement, you've heard of it … What is it called?! I forgot what it's called" she cried. "I'll be right back. Let me go look it up in the book in my office. I know what it's called. I can't believe I can't remember!"

As she ran out to her desk to confirm the name of a supplement, I laughed and thought, *I really like having a doctor who knows what it feels like to be me, but who is capable of healing me.*

We have a great Physician who knows what it feels like to be "us" yet is capable of healing us.

How does the writer of Hebrews describe Jesus? (See Heb. 4:15-16.)

Jesus is our High Priest who identifies with our weaknesses. He has felt our pain and endured our temptation. He offers far more than sympathy and expertise. We have a powerful, great Physician who gives the sweetest gift—*empathy*.

Write what you think empathy is and what it means to empathize.

To have empathy is to understand or identify with someone; to care about, deeply relate to, and enter into their situation or feelings.

Do you think Jesus can empathize with your difficult situations? Why?

Can you think of a situation Jesus faced during His earthly life that gives evidence He knows what you're feeling? If so, jot it down here. (Psst! If you don't know the stories of Jesus that well, no problem. Just call your Bible study buddy and ask her if she knows one that applies to your situation.)

Though there are myriad stories of Jesus facing pain, hunger, temptation, rejection, fatigue, and all the other trappings of humanity, we know He can empathize with your pain simply because our Messiah was to be a suffering servant.

How does Isaiah 53:3 describe Messiah Jesus?

Have you ever felt despised or rejected?

Jesus knows how that feels. He can empathize.

> Remember from school verbs are action words. Read Isaiah 53:4 and note the verbs. What did Jesus "do"?

> What grief do you bear? Jesus bears that grief with you.

> What sorrow do you carry? Jesus carries that sorrow with you.

My friend, He was oppressed and afflicted. He was acquainted with grief—He knew what it felt like. He still does. Jesus is not the cold, distant Physician who won't make eye contact with your questions and suffering. He's not the detached expert who hurries out of your pain.

In His humanity, Jesus chose to patiently walk our roads, feel our pain, and cry our tears. But, in His Deity, He has the power to deliver us when His authority and compassion deem it best. My friend, He cares. He knows what it feels like to weep, to feel pain and sorrow. Jesus also knows how to reach us in our pain with His compassion.

Let Him reach you. Ask Him to enter your circumstance and show you He cares because He does. And, Sister, so do I.

Sometimes life doesn't make sense; sometimes even faith doesn't seem to make sense. But God can fill those missing pieces with something far better than answers. He fills that void with Himself. Ask Him to do that for you today.

Well done. You finished the first week. I pray you have seen and been reminded that God cares deeply for you, Sister. Things are beginning to take shape. I'm proud of you.

1. "Wings quotes," *Brainy Quotes* [online, cited 13 April 2012]. Available from the Internet: *www.brainyquote.com*
2. Thayer and Smith, "Greek Lexicon entry for Anoche," *The New Testament Greek Lexicon* [online, cited 13 April 2012]. Available from the Internet: *www.biblestudytools.com*

Group Session 2

Video Notes

God's _____ of _____ was always perfect.

We're the _____ _____ who needs God.

Conversation Guide

1. The Israelites only noticed they lacked meat when God provided manna. What perceived "lacks" tend to take your focus off of God's provision?

2. How might you demonstrate to God that He alone is your portion?

3. Share with the group specific manna (provisions) with which God has gifted you in recent months—even those that seemed more bitter than sweet.

DOWNLOADS
• •
Video and audio sessions are available at *lifeway.com/jenniferrothschild*

Jennifer's freebie "Peace Giving Promises" for your missing pieces available at *JenniferRothschild.com/MP*

week two

God, Are You Fair?

When I was a little girl in church, I remember singing the beautiful hymn "Fairest Lord Jesus." I loved the melody and took innocent solace in the words.

Fairness was really important to me as a child. I didn't want my brothers to get more candy than me or stay up later than me—I just wanted everything to always be fair! It was a relief to think that Jesus was described in that hymn as the most fair.

I clearly didn't understand the hymn writer was referring to Jesus as the other definition of the word—beautiful, lovely, fair. Even so, could He be described as the most fair … just? When bad things happen to Christians, is it because He really isn't as fair as we'd hoped? Hmm …

In the summer of 2010, my hero, Joni Eareckson Tada was diagnosed with breast cancer. I was so upset and thought, *She doesn't deserve that pain. She's been in a wheelchair since she was a teen. Isn't that enough suffering? She has served God so faithfully even within her disability. That just doesn't seem fair that God would now let her get cancer.*

I compared Joni to others and thought, *That's just not fair. She's earned no cancer.* Have you ever felt that way?

I don't know anyone who has ever read the Book of Job and not thought, *now, this just isn't fair.* We kinda feel like a little suffering is fine, but once you've met the Christian quota for suffering, it just isn't fair for you to get more piled on. Don't we as Christians deserve God's protection, blessings, and healing?

This week, we will explore God's apparent unfairness. We will discover that He is just, not fair.

Day 1 God's "Just," Not Fair

I wish the Bible had a parenting appendix with a remedy for each potential situation. For example, "If your child talketh backeth disrespectfully, giveth him four minutes in time out for each word spoken." Or, "If your son and his friends throweth slime all over your basement at his 13th birthday party …"

I'm sure the inspired appendix would offer the perfect response for such a desecration. Phil and I were on our own dealing with our slime-covered basement.

The sleepover was fun for Clayton and his friends. They'd seen movies, gone to an arcade (where one of the boys won a jar of green slime), and eaten several pizzas. We left them in the basement at about midnight. We heard typical sounds from the subterranean sanctuary as the night waned—laughing, Nerf guns shooting, bass pounding video games, and then, around 3 a.m., quiet.

Saturday morning, they headed out for basketball. That's when Phil went downstairs and discovered the real source of the noise during the night. It wasn't Nerf guns; it was a slime war of monumental proportions. Green gunk was all over our basement. The mantel, the couch, the rug, the pool table, boys shoes, and pizza boxes, all smattered with sticky pea green glop.

In disbelief, Phil questioned the boys. They confessed to the slime war. Phil tried to wash out the stains. It was obvious it would be a lengthy project. So Phil marched upstairs and gathered the boys. "Men," he said, "I planned to wash my van today, but now I won't have time because I must clean the slime from my basement. So, instead of playing basketball, you'll need to finish the party by washing our van." The boys were quiet, except for our son who moaned. Out marched the green teen terrors, sponges and buckets in hand.

> OK, you've heard my story. What story of your own child-rearing would you share over a cup of French roast? If you don't have children, I bet you've still got a story.

An experienced negotiator, Clayton argued how unfair it was to make them wash the van instead of just cleaning the basement. We explained how much easier washing the van was for them than detoxing the basement was for Phil.

We had very different interpretations of what was fair. Unfairness is often a matter of perspective, isn't it?

What in your life or in our world seems unfair to you?

Do you ever feel God isn't fair? Why or why not?

If you sometimes struggle with what seems to be the unfairness of life—or even God—you're not alone. Jesus tells a story about just that. Turn to Matthew 20:1-7.

How much were the first-hired, morning workers to be paid (v. 2)?
○ an hourly wage
○ one denarius for the day
○ what the landowner deemed right

Now circle how much the additional workers were promised (v. 4).

During the 6th, 9th, and 11th hours the landowner hired more laborers and sent them into his vineyard (see vv. 5-7). Now that you have the gist of the story; not all the laborers did the same work but they all got paid the same. Does that seem unfair to you? I'll admit it does to me.

Put yourself in the workers' place. How would you feel if that happened to you?

Disrespected, slighted, and frustrated are just a few of the feelings I would have if that happened to me. We just want to be treated fairly, don't we?

What do you think it means to be fair?

The dictionary defines *fair* as *marked by impartiality and honesty: without self-interest, prejudice, or favoritism.* At first thought, the wage situation doesn't seem fair because all the workers weren't treated equally. But, my friend, fairness and equality are not synonymous. We must guard ourselves against the misnomer of determining God's fairness based on what we perceive as equal treatment.

I've met people who've been healed, yet I have not been healed. Does that mean God isn't fair because He hasn't treated all His children equally when it comes to healing? What if the real question isn't "Is God fair?" What if we should be asking "Is God just?" Here's a potentially radical thought—what appears to be unequal treatment can be just. When you consider your circumstance, do you feel God is treating you with inequality? Can inequality be just?

In verse 11, the workers grumbled against the owner because they thought they weren't treated equally. If the morning workers had based their response on the master's justice rather than their view of fairness, they wouldn't have grumbled.

However, rather than focusing on the word of the master, they focused on the worth of the men's work. They compared.

In your difficult situations, have you ever compared your circumstance to others' or your pain to others' pain? If so, what was the result?

When I compare, my pain becomes the biggest thing in my life. I hold it up to others and focus on me, myself, and why. Comparing is a deeply subjective measure of fairness and it leads to resentment, self-pity, anger, and all sorts of other damaging reactions. When we contemplate the question of fairness, it's usually a self-centered inquiry because we ask, "Is this fair to *me*?" When we ask the question of justice, it is a God-centered inquiry, "Is God right in all His ways?"

Here's the real question: in Jesus' story, was the master just? Read Matthew 20:13.

Did the master lie? ○ Yes   ○ No

He gave exactly what he promised; the master was just. He did not lie. God is just. But, does He ever lie? Can He?

What do Numbers 23:19 and Titus 1:2 both say about God's character?

God does not, cannot, and will not lie.
If He did, He would cease to be just.

It would have been grossly unjust if the master promised one denarius and gave half of one or none at all. It would have been deeply unjust if the master made false promises or lied, but He didn't.

God is just even when He doesn't seem fair.

> **Choose a promise below that will remind you of God's just character.**
> **Write it on an index card to memorize.**
> **God's way and work is perfect; He is faithful to me. Deuteronomy 32:4**
> **God is right and just; He will be my shield and refuge. Psalm 18:30**
> **God doesn't change; I won't be consumed. Malachi 3:6**

"The LORD is righteous in all His ways and gracious in all His acts" (Ps. 145:17). Trust His promise to you for He doesn't lie. Choose to "take Him as He is" and trust His just character acting on your behalf. The laborers may not have understood the landowner's motive, methods, or the meaning of his actions, but what matters most is the master was faithful to his promise.

We may not always understand God's motive, methods, or meaning behind His actions either. But, we see He is faithful to His Word. He is just in the way He responds to each of His children.

My friend, rest today in His just, righteous, and merciful character.

A piece of wisdom from an Egyptian proverb:
*"Is it not in mercy, then, that
sorrow is allotted unto us?"*

Day 2 Undeserved Grace

"This isn't fair!" a disgruntled little boy argued in the checkout line behind me. I don't know what he thought he deserved but he clearly wasn't getting it! "You're right this isn't fair," his daddy replied, "Fair is the place with merry-go-rounds, funnel cakes, and cotton candy, and this ain't it!"

I laughed at his clever response and thought about what is fair.

Often we say, "This isn't fair," based on what we think we deserve. If we suffer, deep down, we begin to wonder if we really deserve it. If you've ever pondered that, you aren't alone. In my pondering, I've come to the conclusion that we don't deserve what we get. Nope. Not at all. See if you agree.

"Miss, where is she seated?"

When the first-class passenger spoke, the flight attendant guiding me down the cramped aisle paused.

Where was I seated? I quipped, "Not up here!"

The flight attendant said my seat was near the back of the plane. Hearing that, the man grabbed his bag and excused himself over the passenger in his row. "I'll take her seat," he told the attendant. "Give her mine."

"Really?" I could hardly believe it. He had paid good money for a first-class ticket. He had the opportunity to enjoy china dishes, cloth napkins, and hovering flight attendants while I was destined for peanuts and leg cramps!

He patted my shoulder as he walked back toward my seat. "I want to," he assured me.

"Thank you," I said as I sank into the lap of airline luxury.

My coach ticket bound me to coach seating—that's what I deserved. But the first-class passenger gave up what was rightfully his to give me what I didn't deserve. I received grace.

Grace is free and undeserved favor. It's unmerited kindness.

What contrasting words in 2 Corinthians 8:9 depict the unfairness of grace?

How does Galatians 3:13 describe grace?

Jesus became poor so we would become rich. He became cursed to remove our curse. My friend, that isn't fair. Remember the disgruntled early morning workers from day 1? They grumbled about the wage received perceiving it as unfair. Do you wonder if they ever considered it was an undeserved privilege to be employed in the first place? They overlooked the grace they were given just to gaze on what they saw as unfair. Ponder that. How often do you consider what you've received from God that you don't deserve?

Go ahead and make a list here. (I bet once you get going, you won't have enough room.)

I have received from God:

I have received from God:

I have received from God:

I have received from God:

When you review your list, can you concede that none of what you wrote is an entitlement? It is what you have received—not what you have achieved.

We've been given so much, but sometimes we stare through the missing pieces of our lives and only see our pain and loss. Questions emerge. We wonder in the deepest part of our souls, *Do I really deserve this difficulty?* But, do you ever ask yourself, *Do I really deserve how good God is to give me grace, forgiveness, peace?* Dwell on this.

My favorite dead author, C.S. Lewis, once wrote, "Goodness is either the great safety or the great danger—according to the way you react to it."[1]

The reaction to the goodness of the landowner who employed the morning workers was not so good. The laborers grumbled about the unfairness. If this parable had a sequel, chances are they wouldn't be hired again. Their reaction to the master's goodness put them in danger of unemployment. As you think about that, ask yourself the following questions.

What kind of reaction to the goodness of God's grace brings you safety?

What kinds of reactions to God's grace bring you danger?

Fill in the following blanks with either safety or danger.
Not noticing grace brings me _____ because I could have a sense of entitlement.
Getting used to grace brings me _____ because I could see myself as spiritually elite.
Being humbled by grace brings me _____ because I see who I am.
Being grateful for grace brings me _____ because I take what I get and don't complain.
Thinking I deserve God's kindness brings me _____ because I can develop pride.
Never accepting God's grace brings me _____ because I live without hope and God.

In the activity you just completed, star which statement(s) best represents your reaction to God's grace in your life.

Rephrase it into a prayer of either correction or protection, depending on what you circled. Pause now and pray or write your prayer on the following page. Be willing to share your prayer with your Bible study buddy or a friend.

Dear Heavenly Father,

Amen

Sometimes, because God has been so generous to us, we fall into an entitle-ment mentality. If we apply entitlement thinking to our suffering, *I don't deserve to suffer,* means we must apply it to our sin too, *I don't deserve to be forgiven.* We want to be entitled to the benefit of God's grace but not be subject to the burden of our sin.

Sister, the point is we can't have one and not the other. Remember, if we really want to experience our own wholeness, we must take God in His wholeness.

May we never sit in first class and complain about the leather chair or the food. We were granted what we did not deserve. Today, if you're mired in difficulty that may feel a tinge unfair, focus on the divine unfairness that will sustain you.

Grace and peace to you Sister.

A piece of wisdom from Charles Spurgeon:
"I am certain that I never did grow in grace one half so much anywhere as I have upon the bed of pain."[2]

Day 3 Mercy Me!

One thing that helps me tolerate and even embrace my blindness is thinking about what I deserve. Though I deal with something frustrating and hard, I'm blessed because even in my darkness, I'm spared from something far worse. Let's explore that today, OK?

What do you think we deserve that we were all spared from receiving?

Because of His holiness, God instituted protocol by which man should approach Him (see Lev. 1–9). One day Aaron's sons freelanced a little. In Leviticus 10 they dishonored God by ignoring the very specific rules for worship in the tabernacle. They offered "unauthorized fire" before the Lord (v. 1). Exactly what Aaron's sons did isn't totally clear to us, but this we know: it wasn't what God required.

Check the result of their careless offering according to Leviticus 10:1-3.
○ God smiled at their creativity.
○ God was disappointed but ignored it.
○ God was just and treated them according to the law.

As much as it pains me to say it, Nadab and Abihu got what they deserved. They fell under the law of the holiness of God, and He acted justly.

Yet, we don't get what we deserve. We all play with unauthorized fire. We show up in His presence with actions and attitudes that affront God's character.

Check the wrong attitudes or actions you have been guilty of presenting before God.

○ hypocrisy   ○ disobedience
○ indifference   ○ unforgiveness
○ pride   ○ self-centeredness
○ a sense of entitlement   ○ not coming before God at all
○ lack of preparation   ○ other:

Simply put, we come before God with sin. Sin shows up as actions and attitudes that don't honor God.

Sometimes Sister, when we're in pain or suffering, we can feel as if it's no big deal to carry a little strange fire of bitterness, resentment, or self-pity. After all, *I deserve a little bad attitude when life is so bad.*

For me, the strange fire I bring is sometimes self-centeredness and other times, anger. Yep. I admit it. They're impure offerings my gracious God does not deserve from me because they're not God-centered attitudes or actions. That strange fire (and its owner) don't deserve to stand before God because it's sin.

What does Psalm 130:3-4 say about our ability to stand before God?

Sinful man cannot stand before holy God on his own terms and live (see Ex. 33:20). Even if you can't think of any unauthorized fire you've carted into God's presence lately, we are by our very nature lawbreakers who deserve what Aaron's sons received.

Read Romans 6:23 and fill in the blank: the wages, or payment of my sin, of my unauthorized fire is _____.

The wages of our sin should be death. But, what does Hebrews 8:12 show we receive instead?

God gives us mercy instead of punishment. If grace is receiving that which we do not deserve, mercy is not receiving what we do deserve. God does not treat us as our sin deserves (see Ps. 103:10). Jesus became sin on our behalf and received the wrath of God so we wouldn't. He paid the penalty for sin that we owed. He took what we deserve so we wouldn't have to.

We don't suffer because we "deserve" it and are not spared from suffering because we "deserve" it. We suffer and are spared because God is sovereign and just. We can't trace the why and why not of who deserves what in this life. But, we can focus on what we do understand—none of us get what we truly deserve because we got mercy we did not deserve instead.

What is the greatest way anyone has ever shown you mercy?

How do you feel toward the person who showed mercy?

As you deal with the missing pieces in your life today, think about how you received mercy from God. Then, consider this thought that helps me: *Your pain is not what makes you need mercy.*

> *Your pain is what God uses to expose the reality that you've been granted and sustained by mercy all along.*

If the classroom of suffering makes us better understand mercy, then I am a grateful student. Even the opportunity to be touched by my frailty in blindness is really a direct result of the mercy of God. My friend, if what we really deserve is hell, then anything else God gives us or spares us from on this side of eternity is a privilege—even suffering.

You and God deal with this together. How do you relate to His mercy as it relates to your suffering? Write out your thoughts, concerns, and questions here. Then, ask God to comfort you and clarify this for you.

Please call your Bible study buddy to pray about this together and jot down what you feel God is showing you.

A piece of comfort from David:
"The LORD is compassionate and gracious, slow to anger and rich in faithful love." *Psalm 103:8*

Day 4 A Proper Response to God

Do you ever think about what is "fair" to God? Do you ever consider what God deserves? Let's go for one more visit to the vineyard in Matthew 20. Those poor guys are still working away. They give us a good example of giving the Master what He deserves. Remember, the workers accused the landowner of unfairness.

> According to verses 11-12, what best describes the morning workers' response to the master's alleged unfairness?
> ○ They thanked the landowner for keeping his promise.
> ○ They resented the late-comers for getting the same pay.
> ○ They humbly received what they got and went away demoralized.
> ○ They grumbled and resented the master.

The master hadn't behaved like they wanted him to. Instead of receiving with gratefulness, they judged his choices. I know you never do that (wink wink, big toothy grin), but let's consider this anyway. We're all capable of grumbling.

> What did the master tell them in verses 13-15?
> I am not being _____.
> I want to give _____.
> I have the right to _____.

The landowner had the right to do as he chose with his money. It was his prerogative for it was his vineyard—his money and his hires.

> How does that picture of the master strike you? Is he right? Why?
>
> Now, think about the landowner being a picture of God. Why does He have the right to do as He pleases?

Isaiah 43:11-13 reminds us that God is God, and when He acts, no one thwarts it. He does as He pleases. We can rest in that potentially terrifying fact as we have the assurance of His just and gracious character. OK, back to the vineyard.

In Matthew 20:15, what did the landowner ask the workers?

How would you rephrase the master's question to the workers as God's question to you concerning your difficult situation in life?

I hear God asking me, "Jennifer, isn't it My right as your Father and the King of the Universe to do as I please with you? Are you judging Me when My ways disappoint you because you are jealous of others or resentful of what I gave you?" When I imagine God's heart in the question of the master, I don't want to complain; I want to bow in gratefulness before Him.

I ask you: Does God have the right to do what He wills with the missing and broken pieces of your life?

When you look at others' lives and perhaps see they seem to deal with less stress, pain, or difficulty, do you judge God for being generous to them? Are you envious of others' seemingly easy lives? Really think about this and then pray about it. God understands your frailty and wants you to be free from anger because anger toward God hurts you as much as it hurts Him.

What does Psalm 37:8 say anger will bring to your life?

Scripture tells us to leave anger behind because it leads to evil—it just makes things worse.

What words describe the kind of life you would like to live?

Does anger lead you to or away from those objectives?

Unless you wrote a list with things like *bitter, discontent, full of illness,* or *resentful,* I would think you said, *no, anger will only lead me away.* Let's be honest. Anger leads to outbursts of depression, bitterness, profanity, defensiveness, isolation, rage, and other undesirable outcomes. I doubt any of those words were on your list. So, does your anger really serve you? Does it change your situation? Does it enhance your relationship with God and others?

Who does your anger really hurt? You? God? Others? Sometimes we assume God can handle our anger, so we can just let it go. We think it's fine to be rash with our mouths and be quick to utter careless words toward God.

> **Really contemplate Ecclesiastes 5:2. What does that verse suggest as a reason to restrain my anger?**

When I think about God in Heaven and us here on earth, I am humbled before Him. I want to show reverence to Him, not complain. I want to let my words be few, grateful, humble, and fitly spoken. He is holy and deserves our respect, not reprimand or anger. (Could anger be just another form of strange fire?)

When we give Him the honor He deserves through our gratefulness, we are the ones who receive peace and life. This freedom is more satisfying even within our pain than it ever could be pain-free but full of anger.

> **How does a grateful response to God over your situation change you and lead to the life you desire?**

> **If you're dealing with anger toward God because of seeming unfairness, rephrase what Asaph wrote in Psalm 73:21-26 into a prayer. He went from grumbling to gratefulness, from anger to adoration. You can too. Do you want to? If so, rephrase his words into a prayer asking God to accomplish that within you.**

In your hard moments, may you be fair to God and give Him praise. Who have we in Heaven but Him?

A piece of my mind:
What honors God, blesses you.

Day 5 Justice Delayed or Justice Denied

I don't know about you, but listening to the news really challenges me to ask the questions, "God, do You really care?" and "God, is this really fair?" It just seems when the innocent suffer, horrible accidents occur, or terror prevails, a just God simply can't be superintending all this chaos.

Can He really be just?

> **What kinds of things in our world make you question God's justice?**

> **For ages, even God's most trusting children have wondered if God could be just. What did David ask in Psalm 82:2?**

> **What did Habakkuk ask in Habakkuk 1:13?**

Both men of faith asked God how long He would show partiality to the wicked and allow the wicked to remain and prevail over the righteous. They each echo our confusion as we worship a just God but still see apparent injustice remain.

Jesus illustrated what injustice looked and felt like as He told the parable of an unjust judge. Read Luke 18:2-5 and imagine you are the widow in the story.

Widows in first-century Palestine knew what it felt like to be totally at risk of unjust treatment. It wasn't like today where a widow may have a pension, life insurance, or even a good job. They were dependent on the good graces of male relatives and people in the community. It must have felt like a pretty unjust lot in life to be a widow in those days. To add to the injustice, the judge who could grant justice ignored the widow in this story.

How do you think you would have felt when the judge kept ignoring your pleas?

○ angry   ○ hopeless   ○ disappointed

○ sad   ○ stupid   ○ afraid

○ neglected   ○ mistreated   ○ other:

Jesus clearly wasn't teaching about a human judge but about God. Sometimes, when our pain remains, we feel ignored by God—the only One who can help us.

In the list of feelings above, circle the words you tend to feel when it seems that God has neglected you.

Why did you choose the word(s) you did?

I feel _____ because _____.

I feel _____ because _____.

I feel _____ because _____.

When our pain remains and our emotions are engaged because of it, we can look to God and wonder how His just nature is showing up in what feels so unjust.

What are we to do? The widow appealed to the judge. Have you appealed to the Judge? Have you appealed to God for healing or deliverance? How has He responded to you?

Circle the word that best describes His response or add your own description.

silent   neglectful   other:

comforting   harsh

responsive   confusing

Is or was God's response thus far what you expected? Why?

How do you tend to continue to appeal or respond to Him?

○ I continue to make my plea.
○ I tend to blame myself for a lack of response.
○ I basically have stoically settled in to wait for Heaven.
○ I've given up on ever getting a response.
○ I'm resting in God's nature and seeking to know Him better.
○ Other:

The widow received a response from the judge to her appeal in
Luke 18:4-5. What was it?

How does the judge's response compare or contrast to how you feel
God is responding to you?

If an unjust judge in the story finally renders justice, how much more will your
just Judge render justice to you? My friend, I get tired of being blind. I know you
get tired of dealing with the stress, sadness, and frustration that come with your
heartache too. It's hard to patiently endure what God allows, but God promises
He will render justice on your behalf. Even if it feels like He isn't responding, He
is and will be faithful to you.

What does Luke 18:7-8 tell us God's response to us will be?

Justice will always and eventually prevail in the high court of the Most High. He
promises us He will be faithful. But, He asks us a question.

Jot down what He asked in Luke 18:8.

Will He find faith on the earth when He returns? More importantly, will He find faith in you and me? To me, that's the bigger question. Not, "Will we be treated fairly?" but "Will Jesus find faith in me?" Do I trust Him to be just even when I don't understand it? Will I be grateful for what I didn't receive and humbled by whatever God has allowed out of His just, merciful character?

My friend, those are questions for which you can have the answer. You decide if God will find you faithful.

> True confession time: Like me, are you sometimes guilty of trying to control other people's business while neglecting to control yourself? Tell me how you do or don't struggle with this.

As much as we'd like to assign a formula to God to control His behavior, we cannot and nor should we. He is I Am. He is not I wish or I feel or I think. We can control what He will find in us though. Anger? Resentment? Entitlement mentality? Gratefulness? Or faith?

> Is faithfulness toward God something that is difficult for you? If so, what makes faithfulness tough for you?

Please share this with your Bible study buddy so she can pray for you and help you grow in your faith. We need each other.

Sometimes faith gets hard because of unanswered questions or God's apparent unfairness or even your own fatigue because you've carried a burden way too long. Sister, God's grace can empower you to remain faithful. Don't just sit despondently in the back of the plane when God has positioned you in first class to soar over your circumstances. Ask Him for grace, humble yourself, and receive it to remain faithful.

The psalmist Asaph, who we visited briefly near the end of day 4, confessed his feet were slipping off the rock of faith when he saw the prosperity of the wicked (see Ps. 73:2-3). We too can get wobbly in our faithfulness because we, like

Asaph, see how mean people seem to have easier lives or like the vineyard workers, we don't receive what we think is fair.

> Complete the following according to James 5:11.
> I am blessed when I _____.
> The outcome of God's dealings with me will always be _____
> and _____.

James reminds us that those who endure are blessed. My friend, hang in there with me. Let's endure until the day we bow before His throne. Don't give up.

Well, you finished another week. I know some days aren't easy and admire you for hanging in there.

> This week's question was, "God, are You fair?" What's your answer?

My answer is, "No and thank You, Jesus!"

A piece of encouragement from Paul:

"There is reserved for me in the future the crown of righteousness, which the Lord, the righteous Judge, will give me on that day, and not only to me, but to all those who have loved His appearing." *2 Timothy 4:8*

1. C.S. Lewis, *Mere Christianity* in Steve Addison, "The great Safety or the great Danger?" *Movements That Change the World* [online], 17 September 2006 [cited 13 April 2012]. Available from the Internet: *www.movements.net*
2. Charles Haddon Spurgeon, *Spurgeon's Sermons on Great Prayers of the Bible* (Grand Rapids, MI: Kregel Publications, 1995), 31. Available from the Internet: *http://books.google.com*

Video Notes

God only gives us what is _____.

God does not give us what we _____.

God is right in _____ _____ _____, yet it may not seem _____.

Conversation Guide

1. Share with the group a time when God did not answer a prayer in the manner you desired. How did He administer grace in that situation?

2. Explain the beauty behind the truth that God does not give us what we deserve. What does this tell you about God?

3. How can you combat the temptation to think that you should have every want met in just the way you desire?

DOWNLOADS

• •

Video and audio sessions are available at *lifeway.com/jenniferrothschild*

Jennifer's freebie "My God Is ..." Character Collection available at *JenniferRothschild.com/MP*

week three

God, Are You There?

Have you ever thought, *If God is really there, why do I feel so alone?* If so, you aren't alone.

Feeling abandoned by God, Gideon said, "If the LORD is with us, why has all this happened?" (Judg. 6:13). Heartbroken because her brother had died, Martha said, "Lord, if You had been here, my brother wouldn't have died" (John 11: 21). We might say, "If You would just give me a sign, I would know You are with me." "If You would just make this trial disappear, I would know You are here." "If You would make today just like my yesterday, I wouldn't be so focused on tomorrow and I could enjoy Your presence." If, if, if.

"If" belongs to a fantasy future or the past; "Is" is a word of the present. God is present in your present, so be present in the present where you are. Be present where He is. Jesus said, "Don't worry about tomorrow, because tomorrow will worry about itself. Each day has enough trouble of its own"(Matt. 6:34).

This week as you contemplate the question, "God, are You there?" Stay present in the present, because God is present in the present.

Day 1 | I Am is Here

Phil and I sat in a coffee shop with our friend David. He shared with us how devastated he was because his wife left him. He was still in shock and utterly heartbroken. Fighting back tears, he said what was troubling him just as much as her absence was that he couldn't "feel God's presence." When something unexpected happens to us, we can feel an aloneness that startles us.

> Have you ever felt that God was absent in your circumstance? If so, what was it like?

> The Sons of Korah knew the feeling. What did they ask in Psalm 44:24?

> In the same chapter, what did they say covers them (see v. 19)?

The Sons of Korah asked God why He was hiding in their time of affliction. They compared their heartache to being covered by "the shadow of death" (NASB).

> What phrase would you use to describe a hard place you have experienced where you felt God's absence?
> O being stuck in a pit of despair
> O traveling on a highway to nowhere
> O holding on to a rope with a frayed knot
> O treading water with no shore in sight
> O alone in a dark room with no window or door
> O other:

Did you notice most analogies we use to describe our hard times usually are singular in nature? They involve just one … us. We feel alone—like God isn't there.

> What contrasting statement of truth does David make about God's presence in Psalm 23:4?

David understood that even when he walked through the valley of the shadow of death, God was with him. A spouse leaving; the death of a child; illness; financial despair; or myriad other hard things feel like that valley. When we walk through such valleys, we often can't feel God's presence—it's just too dark.

That feeling of God's absence reminds me a little of blindness—talk about walking in shadows. Blindness makes it impossible to determine someone's presence if they're still or silent. That can make me feel distant, lonely, or isolated. How strange that I feel those emotions even when someone is right there with me. We can feel the same way about God—distant from Him, isolated from Him, and lonely even though He is right there. In the dark, I can feel alone but my feelings offer no reliable confirmation that I actually am alone.

If someone tells me they are there, then I just have to trust they are. I sure don't want to simplify the profound nature of God nor do I want to seemingly dismiss the pain you may suffer from feeling the absence of God, but my friend, sometimes you just have to trust He is there. Accepting God's omnipresence is a matter of faith; it's that simple … and it's that hard.

> **Let's see what God says about Himself. Turn to Jeremiah 23:23-24. What three questions does God ask to confirm who He is?**
>
> 1.
>
> 2.
>
> 3.
>
> **Now, rephrase the questions God asked into "I am" statements that reflect what God is saying about Himself. God says:**
>
> 1. I am:
>
> 2. I am:
>
> 3. I am:

God claims He is near to all, able to be everywhere so no one can hide from Him, and that He fills every piece of space that surrounds us. He is not subject to or bound by any limitation of space. He is there with you right now. But, even so, you may not feel He is. I know that's hard to grasp. So, try this …

> **Complete the sentence: God's presence is like**

Now, don't worry. I know you're not making a doctrinal statement. We're just trying to make a present reality of something we've probably never pulled up close to our hearts. We have to use words, even knowing our words will fall short. If you had trouble finishing that sentence, don't worry, so did I. I couldn't think of one simile, not even one word that fully represents His presence.

I was really struggling with the concept that God is everywhere. The theological term is *omnipresent*. *Omni* is from the Latin word *omnis* meaning "all." *Present* means *at hand* and *in attendance*—the opposite of absent.[1] The actual word doesn't appear in the Bible, but the concept is everywhere in Scripture.

Yet, even that big, smart-sounding word doesn't do justice to the huge concept. God is everywhere with all His being, with everyone at all times. So, I asked my friend Lisa to finish the sentence.

"God is like air" she said.

"Air? Did you just think of that?!" I asked, surprised she had such a quick, good, and profound answer.

"Yes!" She laughed. "Air is everywhere in our daily lives. We can't go anywhere that it is not. Each of us breathes it."

Think about it. Air is what we all need to survive. We have different languages and skin colors, but we have air in common. It is everywhere. It is invisible and most times, we don't even think about our need for it.

Air is perceptible when it comes in gusts or gentle breezes, a cyclone or when it rustles leaves on a tree. We notice air when it's blustery on a wintery day or swollen with humidity in July.

We can easily think about God's omnipresence in the way we think of air because He is as near and essential as air—our native breath. Not surprisingly, God's name suggests something very similar. In the Old Testament, a name explained a lot about the person who bore it. God's name communicates who He is.

Write what God says His name is in Isaiah 42:8.

God says His name is "The Lord." The original name of God rendered in our Bibles as "Lord" is the Hebrew Tetragrammaton, YHWH.[2] It's used several thousand times in Scripture. God first revealed His name to Moses in Exodus 3:14.

How did He describe His name?

The name may have originated from the Semitic root הוה (hawah) or היה (hayah) meaning "to be" or "to become." It denotes a present, active God.[3]

Out of deep respect for the Lord, it came to be considered blasphemous to even utter the name of God. The name was only written and never spoken. This resulted in the original pronunciation being lost. Many scholars believe the most ancient script, YHWH, could also denote "breath" or "life" in its simplest reference. The word "breath" or "live" may have been fused in thought with "I Am" or "to be," resulting in a meaning similar to "Life-giver" or "Creator."[4]

Modern scholars have come to transliterate YHWH as *Yahweh*, which is used in the Holman Christian Standard Bible translation. In Deuteronomy 30:20 Yahweh declares, "He is your life."

How did Paul describe the ever present God in Acts 17:28, "In Him we _____, _____, and _____."

Yahweh is life. He is I Am. He is as present as the air you breathe. He is as near as the very air that surrounds you—only nearer. He is there even though you can't see or feel Him. He is essential to your life. He is your life. He is I Am.

Take a moment right now and inhale deeply and as you do, breathe in His name, "Yahweh." He is as present as the air you just breathed. Now, exhale and as you do breathe out His name, "Yahweh." He is I Am, and because "He is," you are.

A piece of insight from George MacDonald:

"Let a man think and care ever so little about God, he does not therefore exist without God. God is here with him, upholding, warming, delighting, teaching him—making life a good thing to him. God gives him himself, though he knows it not."[5]

Day 2 Hide and Seek

When I was a girl, we had a white toy poodle named Cannoli. I don't know why her former family named her after an Italian pastry. Whoever named her before we adopted her must have thought she reminded them of that yummy filling. Cannoli was a puffy, fluffy ball of white fur. She was adorable, but she didn't look like a traditional poodle. So, one day, my mom decided to restore dignity to her breed and groom her to look like the refined gal she was meant to be.

After Cannoli's shaving, cutting, and pampering, Mom called us kids to see how pretty she looked. The door opened; we squealed; the dog darted past us and buried her head under the couch. Her well-groomed behind and her cotton ball tail shivered as they stuck out. We pled, but she wouldn't pull her head out.

"She's hiding," Mom explained. "She's embarrassed, and she thinks because she can't see you, you can't see her!"

Poor puppy—she liked her fur coat and not her sleek shave. Cannoli's logic makes me laugh until I think about how similar mine is to hers. If I can't see God, I wonder if He can see me. But, is that line of thinking remotely true? Let's look at three things today that may make us feel God isn't there or can't see us.

1. Shame

> Below circle the four action words the psalmist uses to ask God to remain with him. Then underline the same words in the next paragraph, my commentary on Genesis 3:8.

"Do not hide Your face from me; do not turn Your servant away in anger. You have been my helper; do not leave me or abandon me, God of my salvation" (Ps. 27:9).

Adam and Eve hid due to their shame; they turned away from God's companionship; they rejected His command; they forsook relationship with God to attain independent thinking.

When God walked in the garden, where were Adam and Eve? (See Gen. 3:8.)

Why did they hide according to Genesis 3:10?

Before this event, the couple didn't know they were naked. Their nakedness and failure made them feel ashamed. God asked who told them they were naked. Satan's goal is to make you feel ashamed and distant from God. Satan will condemn you. The Holy Spirit will convict you.

How would you describe the difference between condemnation and conviction?

Both Paul and Peter recall the point of Isaiah 28:16, "Everyone who believes on Him will not be put to shame" (Rom. 10:11; see also 1 Pet. 2:6). Call your Bible study buddy and talk about this. If the Holy Spirit tells you you're naked, it is not so He can shame you; it's so He can cover you.

Why wasn't Paul ashamed according to 2 Timothy 1:12?

Paul put full trust in Christ and was convinced God was able to guard what had been entrusted to him. My friend, a direct link connects a lack of shame and an abundance of trust in God. Really think about this. Ask God's Spirit to teach you this truth in your deep place. If the Devil tells you you're naked it's so he can shame and condemn you. Let God cover you with His forgiveness and restore you to His companionship.

2. Suffering

In Psalm 6:2-4, the psalmist is miserable. He mentions several problems. What are they?

What does he beg God in verse 4?

The psalmist asks God to return to him. He felt the absence of God in his present suffering. I feel that way too sometimes. Do you? I think it's because I am so aware of my personal pain. It can grow so big in my world that everything else—including God's presence—seems to shrink. Perhaps it's a matter of our perspective, not God's presence?

Consider this thought and ask God for His guidance as you look into your own life. Is it true for you? Jot down a prayer to Him.

Dear Lord,
I feel _____.
I know _____.
I confess _____.
I believe _____.
I want _____.
I need _____.
You are _____.
Amen.

Many associate the presence of suffering with God's absence. How could this happen if He is really with me? We will deal with this more tomorrow.

3. Sin

Though God is omnipresent, we can become separated from Him through loss of intimacy. Isaiah 59:2 says "Your iniquities have built barriers between you and your God, and your sins have made Him hide His face from you so that He does not listen." In the tradition of Hebrew poetry the two parts of the verse may simply mean the same thing, but they seem to have a different point of emphasis. The first portion seems to point to sin causing our blindness to God while the second portion to His separation from us.

How would you say our sins erect barriers that prevent our seeing God?

Apart from the saving work of Christ, how do our sins erect barriers that keep God from us?

From Isaiah's perspective before Christ, sin separated two ways: subjectively in us (psychologically) and objectively in God. Christ experienced this awful separation during His crucifixion when, on our behalf, He took upon Himself the full penalty of our sins (see Isa. 53:4-5; Mark 15:34). I wonder what was worse for Christ; receiving God's wrath or the removal of God's presence? Jesus bore that horrible separation from God's presence as He bore our sin. He endured that so you and I would never have to. Christ has paid the objective price for our sin. As God's children nothing can now separate us from the love of Christ (see Rom. 8:35-39). Objectively, God will not abandon us. Subjectively, we can "feel" abandoned when we let sin destroy our intimacy with Him.

> If you have some sin you're holding on to, is it worth the isolation and distance you feel from God? Why or why not?

> What does Acts 3:19 say will be the result of repentance from sin?

Wouldn't you enjoy times of refreshing in God's presence? That is so much more gratifying than the temporary buzz of sin.

> What do the following Scriptures say you gain by repenting from sin and being restored to a more full understanding of God's presence?

> 2 Corinthians 3:17—I can have _____.

> Psalm 16:11—I can have _____.

I want that joy and freedom, don't you? My sweet puppy hid; she couldn't see us so she thought we couldn't see her. Though she hid, I saw her. She couldn't see me but I was there begging her to come out. Shame, suffering, and sin often make us want to hide or make us feel like God is hidden from us. But, come out sweet Sister. He sees you. He is with you.

A piece of truth:
"Where can I go to escape Your Spirit? Where can I flee from Your presence? When I wake up, I am still with You." *Psalm 139:7,18*

Day 3 If You had been here, then …

Have you ever thought, "If God had been here …"? We often create if/then scenarios to explain why things happen or don't happen. If God had been there, then that accident wouldn't have happened. If God was present, then this evil and sorrow wouldn't be going on. Yet, we know God is everywhere—omnipresent. So, if He is there, why doesn't His presence protect us and prevent suffering?

Lazarus's sister Martha had similar thoughts when it came to the suffering and death of her brother. What did Martha say to Jesus in John 11:21? If_____ then _____
_____.

Is Martha's statement to Jesus true? Why or why not?

She believed Jesus' presence could protect and provide power. She knew He could touch Lazarus and heal him. He had done it for others; He could do it for her. That is true. But, consider this: is it a complete or thorough statement of truth? Does her statement reveal that she was limiting God's power to His physical presence? Maybe so, and here's another question.

Could Lazarus have died with Jesus right there with him, holding his hand? If so, why?

"If You had been here …" was looking back and speculating. It conjures up a scenario that we don't know is true. In verses 23-24, Jesus directed Martha to look toward truth. He didn't have her look back or speculate but to look to truth.

What did He tell her in verse 25?

Jesus told her, "I am the resurrection." He is not the I think or I assume. He is I Am. Oh dear Friend, if/then scenarios never bring us comfort. We don't know if our "if" really happened the "then" would automatically follow. You may have someone dear to you who you ask the "if" question about; you may be one who feels "if God had been here with me, then …" The hard truth is you really don't know. None of us do. We feel, we think, and we speculate. But, we don't know.

Don't fill in the missing pieces with speculation. Recognize that God is with you; He always has been and He always will be. He may have allowed tragedy just like He allowed Lazarus's death. As you cry, so does He. Take comfort in His tears.

If you have buried a fellow believer, then be comforted to know He says to you—just like Jesus said to Martha—"Your brother will rise again" (v. 23; see also 1 Thess. 4:16).

How might 2 Corinthians 5:1-7 renew your perspective and give you some real hope?

To be absent from the body is to be present with the Lord. Someday there will be a glorious resurrection (see Acts 24:15).

Do you have some if/then statements you need to get rid of? If so, what are they?

if	then

If/then statements are based on our logic. We often create them to compensate for the mystery of God's action or supposed inactivity. But, Sister, they are myths. God is mysterious. Don't create a myth to try to solve the mystery of who He is and His ways. Guard yourself against the urge to fill in those missing pieces with your own logic.

I found that Scripture uses the idea of if/then often, but it uses it in very different ways than thinking "If God did _____, then I would be happy." Scripture says things like, "If God is for us, who is against us?" (Rom. 8:31), and "We will reap at the proper time if we don't give up" (Gal. 6:9).

What does Deuteronomy 4:29 promise and under what condition?

How does the if/then statement in Psalm 66:18-19 empower us rather than leave us passively waiting for God to do what we want Him to do?

How does 2 Timothy 2:12 provide an if/then scenario that you can really count on?

Would you say the conditional statement in John 8:36 was better or worse than getting your way with an "If God would only do _____" scenario? Why?

The Bible gives us if/then scenarios we can count on. Let's not let our speculations of how we would be happy if only situations take the place of depending on His certainties. In John 11:26 Jesus said, "Everyone who lives and believes in Me will never die—ever. Do you believe this?"

How about you? Do you believe Jesus' promise? Notice I didn't ask if you believed in the promise, do you believe His promise?

Our hope is fixed on the promise that God will do as He says.

Write the truthful if/then statement you need most on an index card or make it the screen saver on your computer. Then meditate on it and memorize it.

If you have missing pieces, fill them with truth.

A piece of comfort:

"May the God of hope fill you with all joy and peace as you believe in Him so that you may overflow with hope by the power of the Holy Spirit." *Romans 15:13*

Day 4 Bethel for Your Soul

Well, we've spent some time this week exploring God's presence. But, I'm most concerned that you experience it. Interestingly, we often experience it best in situations that seem the worst. Pour some coffee and consider this story with me.

In 1851 a group of British missionaries to Tierra del Fuego was stranded in the bitter cold waiting for their supply ship to arrive. Unfortunately, it arrived too late and they all died from cold and starvation. One of the missionaries was a surgeon named Richard Williams. He kept a journal and on April 18 he wrote, "Poor and weak as we are, our boat is the very Bethel to our soul for we feel and know that the Lord is here."[6]

He described the place of their starvation as a "Bethel" to them. What an interesting description of a place of barrenness and despair.

Do you know the meaning of the word *Bethel?* Read Genesis 28:10-19 and let's see what it means and where it comes from.

> **In verse 16, when Jacob awoke from his dream-filled sleep, what did he say about the place he slept?**

At first glance, a cold, hard plot of land doesn't seem like a place God would be. But, consider your hard place.

> **Is the Lord there in your difficulty? How is it possible for God to be there and you not know it?**

**God is everywhere—with me and with you—
and often, we just don't recognize it.**

What is your response to the truth that God is everywhere?

What did Jacob say about the truth that God was there in verse 17?
- ○ How interesting is this place.
- ○ How uncomfortable is this place.
- ○ How awesome is this place.

Jacob was struck with reverence and awe. He described the place as awesome. Yet, don't forget he had just awakened with a stiff neck and sore back from sleeping on the ground with a rock as his pillow. If you have had to sleep in a similar way, would you describe that place as "awesome"?

We wouldn't normally describe that kind of sleeping arrangement in any positive way, but the accommodations weren't what made it awesome.

Jacob described that place as awesome and named it Bethel for he had experienced God's presence there. It was "none other than the house of God" (v. 17). Sometimes the hard places of life make us realize we are in Bethel—God is there.

What in your life could you call Bethel? A hospital room? A funeral service? Think about a hard place where you really experienced the presence of God and tell me about it.

I recognized my soul was in Bethel when I had a biopsy after some suspicious mammograms. Of course, I felt concerned; every waking minute my feelings moved between "what if" and "it is well." I felt nervous when I arrived for the test, but I call it Bethel. It may have been on an examining table surrounded by sterile tools and machinery, but it was Bethel for me because I knew God was right there.

You may not have a Bethel experience in your life yet, but your very soul is Bethel. He is with you.

Perhaps we can't detect God's presence when we are in barren and hard places because we live independent from Him on most days. (Ouch! That stings. Sorry.) I mean, we can't observe or feel His presence in times of trouble because we don't recognize His presence in times of comfort and peace.

Maybe we struggle when life gives us missing pieces because we live apart from God. We don't recognize the astounding reality that He is with us. So, when suffering comes, it isn't that it removes us from God's presence, but it reveals we have not really noticed His presence all along.

I hate to do this to you, but please humor me. Review the previous three paragraphs and on the scale below rate yourself on recognizing God's presence.

....

constantly aware of Him   wrapped up in me

A hard piece of ground and a rock for a pillow can be a miserable experience or it can be the discomfort that positions you to experience the presence of God—a very Bethel for your soul.

The great Christian theologian Augustine knew what it felt like to finally realize God was there with him though he had been disinterested or unaware. He wrote:

Too late have I loved you, o beauty so ancient and young; too late have I loved you! And behold you were inside of me, and I was outside of myself, and that was where I was looking for you.[7]

Can you relate to Augustine's words? If so, describe.

Where does this message meet you? Do you recognize His presence with you during good and ordinary times? Does what feels like God's absence really show you haven't noticed His presence all along? If so, my friend, He longs to abide with you. Augustine said it was "too late" but it's not. Just ask Jesus. He says, "If anyone loves Me, he will keep My word. My Father will love him, and We will come to him and make Our home with him" (John 14:23).

Jesus wants to make His home with you and the address of your soul Bethel. Are you willing to invite Him in through loving Him and keeping His Word?

> Today, how can you invite Him in by loving Him? What would that look like?

> How can you invite Him to abide with you today by keeping His Word? Which of His words or commandments do you most need to keep today?

Ask God to abide with you today. He will. He will because He is I Am.

A piece of truth:
"My presence will go with you, and I will give you rest."
Exodus 33:14

Day 5 Lessons from Emmaus

One Sunday morning after worship, Phil turned to me and said, "Jennifer, I want you to meet Yakov Smirnoff." I turned in my pew toward Phil and laughed, "Very funny." You see, Phil is ever pulling some kind of prank, usually random and nonsensical. So, I admired his imaginativeness in creating this one by pulling out a name from the past. Yakov was a Russian-born comedian who I had seen on TV. He always made jokes about the KGB and had a laugh that can't be imitated. "Leave me alone," I snapped at Phil as I turned to visit with someone beside me.

"No, Jennifer, really …" I felt a tinge of awareness as if Phil could actually be serious. Stranger things have happened, I guess. Yakov could be at my church, in the pew behind me just as easily as I could run into Brad Pitt at my local Walmart.

"I won't believe it unless I hear him laugh" was my clever retort. Clever I thought until I heard this guttural, raspy sound like an asthmatic seal choking up cotton balls. It was him. There's no mistaking the laugh of Yakov Smirnoff.

I was both embarrassed and enchanted. He was so whimsical and kind. But, who would have thought? You just never know who is right there with you, near you, around you … do you?

The reality of God's omnipresence is that He is everywhere, but He can show Himself to be with us in ways and places we least expect. His presence is personal just as it was on a dusty road to Emmaus. Luke tells of a walk from Jerusalem to Emmaus which crescendos with an appearance by Jesus Himself. Depending on the disciples' pace, the walk could have taken anywhere between an hour to three hours. For a couple of guys, these were very chatty. They were in a deep conversation.

> In Luke 24:14-19, what were they discussing?
> O the price of fishing nets
> O everything that had happened the last few days
> O how much they needed new sandals
> O the next Roman election

What had happened that they were referring to?

In the midst of their conversation about Christ's crucifixion, Christ Himself approached. The Greek word in verses 14-19 for *approaches* is *eggizo* meaning to "draw or come near to, to approach."[8] Jesus is Immanuel—God with us. He is the One who draws near to us.

Jesus interrupts their conversation and asks what they're talking about. (Note that it's always a good idea to be willing to be interrupted by God's presence.) Cleopas can't believe this stranger doesn't know so he begins to describe who Jesus is and what He had done.

How does Cleopas describe Christ in 24:19b?

The disciples describe Jesus as a prophet, powerful in word and deed. But, their conversation also revealed that they didn't expect a Resurrected Lord.

If Jesus were to draw near while you and your friend were talking, what would He be likely to hear?
○ a spiritual conversation   ○ talk about family
○ gossip   ○ discussion of my wants
○ talk of shopping   ○ other:

What does your conversation reveal about your expectation of God's presence? Does the nature of your talk reveal an awareness God is with you? This would be a good topic of conversation between you and your Bible study buddy the next time you share coffee.

Do you expect Him? He is Immanuel—God with us.

The disciples didn't expect Christ, that's for sure! But, the stranger began to astonish them with His teaching.

What did Jesus do before He taught them? See Luke 24:25-27.

It's rough, but He rebuked them for their unbelief. He calls them "foolish" (NIV), using the Greek adjective *anoetos*, which is a compound word, formed from two words meaning *without, not* and *understanding, perception*.[9] Jesus wasn't hurling insults. He was simply acknowledging that His disciples should know these things about Him. He continues by starting with Moses and teaching them all that pertains to Himself as Messiah.

> **How did the disciples later describe their reaction to this amazing encounter in verse 32?**

Has your heart burned within you because of God's presence and Word? The next time you feel that soul excitement or like you may burst from what you're learning from Scripture consider that kind of heartburn indicates God is with you.

Christ chose not to reveal Himself to the men on the road, but even though they weren't aware of His identity, He was with them. He was walking with them and teaching them. The same applies to you and me my friend. We may not always recognize Him, but He is with us.

God is present in His Word. Our heart burns when we recognize it, but we are guaranteed a God visitation in another situation as well.

> **What does Matthew 18:20 promise and under what condition?**

When you gather with your Bible study buddies, He is there. The writer of Hebrews has something to say about that.

> **Rephrase and amplify Hebrews 10:25 into a positive command.**

I rewrote the passage this way: join together; hang out frequently; don't miss a chance getting together with your fellow believers. Jesus is there when you commune and share companionship with other believers.

The origin of the word *companion* interests me. It's from the Latin *companionem*, which consists of *con* meaning *with* and *pan* meaning *bread*. A companion is someone with whom you "break bread."[10] Return to Luke 24:28-30.

As the disciples approached the village, what did Jesus do?

Why do you think Jesus acted like He was going further?

Perhaps Jesus pretended He was going further so the disciples would have a chance to pursue relationship with Him. Perhaps it was simply good manners; a visitor would never invite himself into someone's home. We don't really know, but I wonder. Either way, I want to be the disciple who says, "Stay with us." Don't you? I want Him to abide with me and share companionship. He will always be a gentleman and never force Himself; He just draws near and gives us opportunity to respond.

What did Jesus do with the bread at dinner according to verse 30?

The host normally took the bread, offered the blessing, broke it, and served to the others.

Why do you think Jesus, as a guest, assumed that role and served?

I don't know either, but Jesus came to serve, not to be served (see Matt. 20:28). Sister, this is God with us. He draws near, interrupts our daily lives, initiates, and serves us. Remember the "divine unfairness" we discussed in week 2? Well, this is it once again.

What happened to the disciples in Luke 24:31?

Do you need a verse 31 moment? Do you need your eyes opened to the very present God in your midst? If so, stop right now and ask Him to do that for you. You may want to write your prayer so you can remember later.

Emmaus teaches us God is there when we don't expect Him. He is there and we don't often recognize Him. He is there when two or three are gathered in His name, and He is there when we commune, breaking bread together.

Why don't you finish up this week by getting together with some of your Bible study buddies and share a meal; companionship; together with bread. Talk together about your questions from the week and your "aha" moments.

Being together with bread also includes being together with *the* Bread of life. Ask Him to lead your conversation. And, where two or three are gathered together in His name, Yahweh is with you.

1. "Omnipresence," *Dictionary.com* [online, cited 13 April 2012]. Available from the Internet: *http://dictionary.reference.com*
2. "Tetragrammton," *The Free Dictionary* [online, cited 13 April 2012]. Available from the Internet: *www.thefreedictionary.com*
3. "Yahweh," Behind the Name [online, cited 13 April 2012]. Available from the Internet: *www.behindthename.com*
4. Arie Uittenbogaard, "Meaning and etymology of the name YHWH," Abarim Publications [online, cited 13 April 2012]. Available from the Internet: *www.abarim-publications.com*
5. George MacDonald, *Unspoken Sermons* (London: Alexander Strahan, 1867), 23. Available from the Internet: *http://books.google.com*
6. "Cape Horn Patagonian News," *The Patagonian News* (September 2003). Available from the Internet: *www.victory-cruises.com*
7. "Quotation by Augustine Of Hippo," *Dictionary.com* [online, cited 13 April 2012]. Available from the Internet: *http://quotes.dictionary.com*
8. Thayer and Smith, "Greek Lexicon entry for Eggizo," *The New Testament Greek Lexicon* [online, cited 13 April 2012]. Available from the Internet: *www.studylight.org*
9. Thayer and Smith, "Greek Lexicon entry for Anoetos," *The New Testament Greek Lexicon* [online, cited 13 April 2012]. Available from the Internet: *www.studylight.org*
10. "Companion," *Online Etymology Dictionary* [online, cited 13 April 2012]. Available from the Internet: *www.etymonline.com*

Group Session 4

Video Notes

God is _____ in our _____.

Gideon did not _____ the presence of God.

"_____" is not a statement of present. "_____" is a statement of present.

God is I _____, He is not I _____ or
I _____.

Conversation Guide

1. What things hinder you from living in the now?

2. Share about a time when you focused on the "if" rather than trusting the presence of God in your present.

3. How might you actively demonstrate to God that you are resting in the reality of His presence?

DOWNLOADS

Video and audio sessions are available at *lifeway.com/jenniferrothschild*

Jennifer's freebie "God is Present" Table Talk Cards available at *JenniferRothschild.com/MP*

God, Are You Aware?

I wish I hadn't turned on the TV that summer morning. I awoke a little later than usual. I knew the kids were still asleep and Phil was already up. So, still lying in bed, I grabbed the remote and within seconds a morning talk show appeared on the screen.

I was just in time to hear an interview with Angelina Jolie. She was introduced as one of the most beautiful women in the world. The interviewer went on to describe how she was starring in a movie where she played a spy. He went on to say something like, "She does her own stunts; she's an amazing mother; she's athletic; she's smart; she's articulate; and she's got a great figure." Whew!

I dragged my very unathletic self out of bed to perform the only stunt I was capable of; walking to the kitchen to pour my coffee! When I arrived with bed head in my faded pj's, Phil greeted me with a cup of coffee.

"Thanks, Honey" I said. Then I asked, "Did you see that piece about Angelina?" He told me he did so I said, "I bet you like her more than me!" He giggled as I recounted how pretty she is, what a great figure she has, how smart she is, what a great mom she is, how athletic she is. I went on and on. I felt insignificant compared to the hot humanitarian I had to digest before breakfast. I felt totally unimportant; like no one, especially God, could be aware of someone like me when someone like Angelina shared the planet.

Have you ever felt insignificant? Have you ever felt like God couldn't possibly be aware of you especially if hard things are going on in your life?

This week, as you consider this question, "God, are You aware?" I want you to do so knowing you are "in-significant." In other words, realize you dwell in the significance of Christ; He is totally aware of you and He has stooped down to make you great (see Ps. 18:35).

Day 1 God Knows It All

Let's play an imaginary game of Jeopardy, OK? I'll go first. "Alex, I'd like the 'Smarter than Me' category for $100."

Alex: "OK, that's a huge category, Jennifer! 'Smarter than Me' for $100—here are your clues: He can process 500 gigabytes, the equivalent of a million books, per second. He can calculate hundreds of algorithms simultaneously to parse human language complexities such as puns. He has 16 terabytes of memory and defeated the all-time Jeopardy champion."

Me: "Who is Watson?"

Alex: "You're right! IBM's Super Computer named Watson is correct, and on that note, we'll be right back."

(*Hum theme music because we're heading into a commercial break, and I will use the 30 seconds to tell you about Watson.*)

Watson is a super computer that performs so fast it can rival the greatest human contestants in Jeopardy. Watson can understand the language of a clue, figure out the intent of a question, comb millions of lines of human language, and return a precise answer—in less than three seconds.[1] Isn't that amazing?! I can't even begin to imagine what is going on in Watson's mainframe. My neurons over-heat and make my brain short-circuit just thinking about such vast knowledge …

(*Hum music again. It's your turn next.*) Producer offstage: "5, 4, 3, 2, …"

Alex: "And we're back!"

You: "Alex," you confidently say, "I'd like the 'Smarter than Everybody including Watson' category for $100."

Alex: "Good choice! Here are your clues: He is the Creator and He is eternal. He knows all things about all people at all times. No one taught Him anything. The apostle Paul once called His knowledge 'unfathomable.' "

You: Who is _____?

OK, that was silly and surely you answered "God." But, you get the point. God knows everything.

That's what we know to be true about God. But, let me ask you this: When it comes to the hard places, the missing pieces in your life, do you feel like God really knows? Often, when life doesn't make sense, somewhere deep down we can think, and even hope, that God just isn't aware. Because, let's face it, if He is aware and He doesn't step in, we can feel even worse.

So, again, do you think God is really aware of everything—every little thing—or just the biggies like wars and famine?

Let's start by establishing if He even claims to know everything.

List below what He "knows."
Psalm 50:11, He knows _____.
Psalm 147:4-5, He knows _____.
Matthew 10:29-30, He knows _____.

He knows the number and names of each star. He knows every sparrow that falls and each hair on your head. He knows every bird of the mountains and every beast in the field.

Would you describe those objects of God's knowledge as "important"? Seriously, do you count the hairs on your head each morning? Do you pull out your telescope and count the stars each night and then go through each one and review their names?

Why do you think God gives us such seemingly unimportant examples of what He knows?

Maybe God wants to dismiss any notion His knowledge is only reserved for what we consider the big or important issues in our lives. God really cares; He is aware. Ultimately, God knows all because His knowledge is innate and inherent. He knows everything by the very essence of His being. An infinite God must possess infinite knowledge.

What questions did the prophet Isaiah ask in 40:13-14 to show God's knowledge? Rephrase the questions into statements.

1. No one _____.

2. He consulted with _____, and no one gave Him

_____.

3. No one _____ Him.

No one has directed God's Spirit or informed Him; He didn't consult with anyone; and no one gave Him understanding. No one taught Him. He is omniscient. It means God is "all-knowing" (omni means all; science means knowledge).[2]

God has perfect knowledge of everything—stars and sparrows; hairs and hurricanes; past, present, and future; what is actual and what is possible.

Which word best summarizes your feelings about God's knowledge? You can choose more than one or even conflicting responses.

○ amazing   ○ confusing
○ troubling   ○ unbelievable
○ comforting   ○ unfathomable
○ hurtful   ○ other:

Why did you choose the word(s) you did?
I chose _____ because _____.
I chose _____ because _____.

How about you call your Bible study buddy and discuss this with her? Ask the Holy Spirit to guide your conversation into all truth. Then, jot down how you feel after talking to her. Did your feelings about the words you chose change? Or did you change the words you chose?

Jot down one insight you gained from your conversation with her.

When I think of God's knowledge, I can't wrap my puny brain around it. His omniscience humbles me, gives me a sense of security yet at the same time makes me a little uncomfortable.

I'll tell you more about that last feeling tomorrow. When Paul thought about God's omniscience, it caused him to make an interesting exclamation.

Look in Romans 11:33. How did Paul react?

He exclaims that not only is God's knowledge and understanding such a treasure, but he meditates over the "depth" of it.

> **Look in a thesaurus or dictionary for synonyms of the word *riches*. Choose three examples.**

Possessions, treasures, assets, and *resources* are a few of the synonyms I found. Paul compares God's knowledge to treasure, a rich resource and an asset.

> **How is God's omniscience a treasure, asset, or resource for you?**

> **Paul goes on to say God's judgments and ways are _____ and _____.**

If they're unfathomable, they're too deep to measure. If they're unsearchable, they're broader, wider, taller, bigger than we can discover. We can feebly attempt to explain God's omniscience but most importantly, I want you to experience the benefits—the depth of the riches—of it.

As you go through the rest of your day, think of something you treasure. Maybe it's the ring on your finger or a gift from someone you love. Ponder the "depth" of that treasure. Ponder why it means so much to you, how you regard it, and so forth. As you do, think of God's knowledge in the same way. Ask God to teach you what it means to have "the depth of the riches" of His wisdom and knowledge as a resource for you.

Now, go walk in the blessings you possess!

Day 2 God Knows Your Name

Sent: Wednesday, October 05, 2011 5:11 AM

"Hi Jennifer,
I am not sure you will receive this msg. you addressing each msg with my name makes me feel so warm and I truly feel that you indeed know me. I love reading yr msg and visit yr website. Indeed very encouraging.
Betsy"

I received Betsy's e-mail while studying about God's omniscience. Betsy's words struck me. They didn't strike me just because of the amount of abbreviations (welcome to the new, grammatically-bankrupt millennium) but because such a small gesture as using her name made such a big impact. The fact I addressed her monthly e-mail newsletter personally made her feel like I knew her. Do you ever wonder if God knows your name?

If we accept God's omniscience, we may think it's so broad that He simply knows "about" us but doesn't really know us.

> In Psalm 8:4 the psalmist asked the nagging question we all wonder. What is it?

We wonder if God really notices us and knows us. Who are we that He would pay attention and be aware of us? That question can be answered with an anthropomorphism. Have you ever heard that impressive word?! OK, here's what it means so you can throw it out at dinner and impress your people. Anthropomorphism means *ascribing human characteristics to God.*

> With what anthropomorphic feature does Proverbs 15:3 describe God? How does it show His vast knowledge?

The writer of Proverbs uses "God's all-seeing eye" to communicate that God knows everything. Assigning God human features simply means using literary devices to help us comprehend God. But, let's be perfectly clear. John 4:24 accurately describes God as Spirit. He does not have eyes, arms, or ears in the same way we have eyes, arms, and ears. We just have to have some way of understanding Him, and assigning characteristics to Him that we can relate to really helps.

Sister, His eye is on you … but, that's not all.

> **What anthropomorphic characteristics are given to God indicating God's awareness of you in Isaiah 49:15-16?**

Isaiah uses the picture of engraving on God's palms because in ancient eastern culture this form of tattoo would be a familiar image. And, in our current culture, tattoos are a familiar image too. Butterflies, boyfriend's names, Bible verses, and all sorts of images are tattooed on arms and ankles. Whether or not you agree with the practice, think about what it represents.

A tattoo usually denotes importance and permanence to the one who bears it. Why do you think God evoked that picture to communicate knowing us?

> **What does that say to you?**

The tattoo on His hand is evidence of His knowledge of us and our value to Him. Can you think of another permanent "puncture" on the hands?

God inscribes peoples' names on His palms, and Jesus bears the ultimate puncture on His hands because you are known and loved. He doesn't just know about you; He knows you.

> **Knowing Jesus' hands bore the scars of nail punctures, what must be the answer to the question David posed in Psalm 8:4?**

Before Jeremiah was formed in his mother's womb God knew he would be a prophet according to Jeremiah 1:5. Galatians 1:15-16 tells us that God set the apostle Paul apart from his mother's womb "so that [he] could preach [Christ] among the Gentiles." God knew Paul would preach to the Gentiles.

Think about it. What did God know about you before you were born? God knew I would be blind and be born in Clearwater, Florida, to precious parents. He knew I would fall head over heels in love with Philip Rothschild and then love our sons, Clayton and Connor, more than I thought possible! He knew I would learn of Him, love Him, and follow Him. He also knew I would love dark chocolate and coffee, avoid sensible shoes, and develop a mad crush on my favorite dead author C.S. Lewis. (Just had to throw that in!)

What did He know about you before you were born? Include facts about you that are both blessings and difficulties.

blessings about me	difficulties about me

The sadness you struggle with, the disappointment you carry, your hard past, the trials you endure … He knew and He knows. Your best memories, your talents, and secret dreams … He knew and He knows. Your relationship or the lack thereof, your body size and shape … He knew and He knows.

How do you feel as you reflect on what He knows about you?

My friend, I know you may have written down some tough feelings because of what you may have endured in your past. It could be hard to admit or embrace God really knew what was happening to you and He still let it happen. I have struggled with that when it comes to my friend Regina's death. I don't understand why God knows all this and still lets it happen. We can theorize, but our hearts aren't satisfied by theological answers. This I do know: God's children don't live by answers, we live by faith. We choose to take Him as He is … not I wish but I Am.

Hannah struggled with a burden that brought her to tears (see 1 Sam. 1:6). What was it?

What did Hannah call God in her prayer in 1 Samuel 2:3?

Hannah, in her barrenness, knew God was aware. When she conceived, she knew God was aware. He knows all. Hannah said, "The LORD is a God of knowledge." Can you pray like Hannah? Acknowledging God is a God of knowledge is acknowledging that what He knew and knows, He allows and redeems.

Write a prayer of acceptance and submission to His all-knowing character.

Dear God,

Amen

My friend, you aren't just another set of chromosomes and DNA roaming the planet. You are a child of God with a special story, a special calling, and a special name. God knows who you are, where you've been, and where you're going.

Pour yourself some coffee or tea and snuggle up with your Bible. Read through Psalm 139 and circle or highlight the word "know" every time you see it. Then read it aloud again and replace every pronoun with your name. Now, Sister, rest in His knowledge.

A piece of insight from Meister Eckhart:
"For however devoted you are to [God], you may be sure that He is immeasurably more devoted to you."[3]

Day 3 Is there anything He doesn't know?

My 2-year-old Clayton and I piled into the backseat of Lori's van. Clayton and Lori's son, Vince, were on their way to Mother's Day Out, and Lori and I were on our way to anywhere—we were just ready to get out. Diaper bags and blankets and books and sippy cups and a million other pieces of baby paraphernalia filled the backseat with them. When we arrived at church, we gathered all of the boys' stuff. Clayton's sippy cup was nowhere to be found.

Note: Clayton is the firstborn son of a firstborn mom who is a daughter of a firstborn mom; this situation was about to become a first-class, first-rate, firstborn nightmare. I picked up blankets and books and shifted bags and parcels but no cup. He crawled around the floorboard; we checked behind his car seat. Stress was rising; concern was growing. I told him we'd borrow one when we got into his classroom. He was really upset. Just then, Lori called out, "I found it!"

Clay grabbed it as I asked, "Where did you find it?"

"Under my seat, I knew it must have rolled there."

Before I could say anything, Clayton announced confidently, "Mommy, Lori is just like Jesus; she knows everything!"

Is that your impression of Jesus? Do you think He knows "everything"?

Often we can trust that God, Yahweh, is all-knowing, but when it comes to Jesus, God in the flesh, some can get a little unsure. After all, though He was fully God, He was fully human … and I can't remember too well these days, but I think humans tend to be forgetful! Could He really be omniscient?

> Let's ask His disciples their opinion. What do they say about Jesus in John 16:30?

Do you agree with the disciples; do you know He knows all things? Faith is your proof that Jesus knows all. But, let's see what Scripture teaches about His knowledge. We will look at four areas of His omniscience.

1. Jesus knew what was.

John 17:5 says Jesus _____.
John 8:58 says Jesus _____.
Hebrews 1:2 says Jesus knew the past because _____.

Jesus existed in eternity past and shared God's glory. He was there at creation—the worlds were made through Him. Jesus is eternal. He knows the past and He knows your past. What in your past are you grateful He knows? Whatever that is, it is part of the depth of the riches of His knowledge. Thank Him.

2. Jesus knows what is.

Jesus was teaching and healing in a house in Capernaum when four men tore off the roof tiles and lowered a paralytic friend into His presence.

What does Mark 2:5 say was Jesus' response to their faith?

How did the watching scribes and Pharisees react to Jesus forgiving sin? (See vv. 6-7.)

What does Mark 2:8 reveal about Jesus' knowledge?

Those poor scribes and Pharisees were busted! Not only could Jesus heal and forgive sin, He could read their minds. He knew what they were thinking.

What similar thing happened in Luke 5:22?

How do you feel knowing Jesus knows your thoughts? Well, depending on what I am thinking I can feel pretty uncomfortable! But, if He knows your thoughts, why try to hide them from Him? Just tell Him what is on your mind and let Him carry the burden for and with you.

3. Jesus knows what will be.

Jesus was eating with His disciples in a second story room. He made two prophecies in Luke 22:21-22. What were they?

Jesus showed He had knowledge of what individual people would do and what events would take place. He indicated He knew He was to be betrayed and knew who was going to do it. Jesus also told His disciples that He was soon to be going as it has been determined.

See what else He knew on that occasion. What did He say to Simon Peter in Luke 22:34 suggesting He knew the future and He knew Peter intimately?

Jesus knew Peter would cave under pressure and deny knowing Him. He knew Peter would falter and later repent.

Jesus knows the future and your future. Are concerned about something in your future? Jesus knows about it and He knows what will be. You can trust Him.

4. Jesus knows what if.

Jesus made a disquieting observation in Matthew 11:21 revealing His omniscience when He predicted judgment on some of the Israelite cities.

After He pronounced His "woes," what did He say that showed He knew the "what ifs"?

He stated that if the miracles, which occurred in their cities, had occurred in Tyre and Sidon, those people would have repented. Verse 23 states something about Sodom, which reveals an unsettling aspect of God's sovereign omniscience. Jesus told them that if the miracles they were privy to happened in Sodom, that city would still remain because evidently they would have responded with repentance and faith.

Jesus knew what people of Tyre, Sidon, and Sodom would have done if they'd had the same spiritual benefits which those Israelite cities had. God's omniscience includes the potentialities and possibilities as well as the actualities.

God knows the "what ifs" and the "what might have beens." This can be both confusing and comforting.

First, the confusing part: If God knew those cities would have responded correctly to His miracles, why didn't He give them that chance? How can He judge them for their sin or for rejecting Him if He knew they would have repented but He didn't give them opportunity? Hmm …

Your thoughts?

I just don't and may never understand some mysteries. But, am I going to trust Him or trust my own understanding? When I don't understand His ways, I look to His character to find clarity.

What do you know about God's character that may give clues to this mystery?

Somehow God's choice is a reflection of His compassionate, just, perfect character. Whew! My brain hurts …

Now for the comforting part. Part of the reason I take comfort in God's omniscience is not simply because *He knows,* but because of *what* He knows. When I miscarried our second child and was filled with grief, God knew. I was comforted He was totally aware. After my tears finally ceased to fall, I realized that my greater comfort was in what He must have known that I clearly can't know. He knows the ifs. What if that sweet baby were destined for a life of sorrow? What if that baby was being protected by being born in Heaven rather than earth? God not only knows the actualities, He knows the potentialities. I don't know what He knows; I just know that He knows. And that is good enough for me.

Let's face it Sister, it has to be. That's all we've got. So, if that's all we've got, God must have decided that it is enough.

Talk with a Bible study buddy and discuss: Is there anything Jesus doesn't know?

(Take your Bible with you and consult Matthew 24:36 if you need a hint.)

Day 4 If He knows, why does He ask?

"Do you have any questions?" My OB doctor asked those fear-inspiring words as he sat across from me. I was pregnant with our first child.

"I don't know enough to know what I don't know so I don't know what questions to ask," I nervously replied.

Have you ever felt the awareness that you know so little you aren't even aware of what you don't know? I suspect we all have. The older I get, the less I know.

When I was younger, I used to think asking questions was a sign of ignorance but actually, it's a sign of knowledge … hmm.

Let's look at questions the omniscient, all-knowing God asked. Was He simply trying to learn or seek information? After Christ's death and resurrection He appeared to His disciples by the Sea of Galilee. Read John 15:17.

> After finishing breakfast, what question did Jesus ask Simon Peter three times in John 21:15-17?

> The first two times Peter responded by telling Jesus what?

> Of course Jesus knew. What do Psalm 139:4 and Proverbs 5:21 indicate about what God knows?

> Peter reminded Jesus that He knew Peter loved Him. The third time, however, how did Peter feel about Jesus asking again (see John 21:17)?
> ○ irritated   ○ confused
> ○ perplexed   ○ offended
> ○ grieved

How do you think you would feel if you were Peter?

I think I too would feel grieved if Jesus kept asking me the same question for which He knew the answer.

What did Peter finally say to Jesus (v. 17)?

Since Jesus already knows everything, I would not only be grieved but perplexed. I think I'd find myself asking, "God, You know everything; You know me, don't You? Why are You asking me this?" Exasperated by his inability to make his point, Peter appealed to Jesus' omniscience, "Lord, You know everything! You know that I love You."

If you stood before Jesus and said "You know everything," how would you finish the sentence? "You know that I _____."

What is the first word that comes to your mind? Love? Need? Neglect? Run from? Trust? Doubt? Why? Be honest.

A year before writing this study, I went through a dark time of depression. I spiraled into a deep place of doubt. It was so painful to admit I doubted God's existence and even the Deity of Christ. But God already knew I was struggling with that. "You know all things; You know I doubt You."

I believed Him enough to tell Him of my doubts even though I wasn't sure He was even real. I was so, so confused and had just enough hope and volition to embrace what I couldn't understand. After several terrifying and hard months, God's grace gently guided me back to the truth that He is not I feel or I think but He is I Am.

If you're struggling with uncomfortable feelings about faith and God, tell Him. He already knows. He knows all things. When you are willing to reveal yourself completely to God, He reveals Himself to you. To isolate yourself from Him just because the missing pieces of your life make no sense is only hurting yourself. Dear Friend, please don't do that. Be real with God, real with yourself, and real with your Bible study buddies.

We play games to keep others from knowing what we struggle with—whether sin or suffering. Some of the Bible study gals are the best at it! Ouch! Sorry Sister, but wouldn't you rather let go of pride and gain freedom?

We get pretty good at fooling most of the people most of the time. We even begin to fool ourselves, but God is not fooled. He knows everything about us.

So, why do you think Jesus asked Peter those questions if He already knew everything? (Read Mark 14:66-72.)

I think Jesus did not ask the questions to find out if Peter loved Him; He asked for Peter's sake. Peter recently denied Jesus and didn't understand why he had done it. He probably doubted his own devotion to Christ and feared he'd never be accepted by God again. Jesus' questions allowed Peter to see what was in his heart. Jesus gave him a chance to reaffirm his love and reassured him of future usefulness. God understood him when he didn't even understand himself. Man, I've been there. Let the omniscient God ask you questions. Be open to His probe. It's because He loves you, not because He wants information or is setting you up for a "Gotcha!" His questions are asked to free and refine you.

Consider the questions He asked below and answer them personally as if He were asking you.

Adam, where are you (see. Gen. 3:9)?

Moses, who are you (see Ex. 3:4)?

Peter, who do you say I am (see Luke 9:20)?

Saul, why are you (see Acts 9:4)?

This whole topic raises an issue both encouraging and threatening. It points us to the fact that God will do for us what we need—no matter how threatening or difficult His actions may be.

Does this thought encourage you or make you apprehensive? Why?

God doesn't ask so He will know; He asks so we will know.

A piece of wisdom from C.S. Lewis:
"Be sure that the ins and outs of your individuality are no mystery to Him; and one day they will no longer be a mystery to you."[4]

Day 5 Forgetful Omniscience

OK Sister; let's finish this week with something sort of puzzling. Just thought I'd warn you in case you need to get a strong cup of coffee before you start. By this time, you've decided if you believe God is omniscient or not. Hopefully, you believe He is (because He is).

So, how about this ... if God really does know all things, why do Scripture writers ask God not to forget? Can omniscience forget?

Hannah, David, and Asaph all begged God not to forget, so when you feel forgotten by God, at least you're in good company.

As you read the following passages, underline words or phrases with which you most identify when it comes to your missing pieces.

"Deeply hurt, Hannah prayed to the LORD and wept with many tears. Making a vow, she pleaded, 'LORD of Hosts, if You will take notice of Your servant's affliction, remember and not forget me, and give Your servant a son, I will give him to the LORD all the days of his life, and his hair will never be cut' " (1 Sam 1:10-11).

"Rise up, LORD God! Lift up Your hand. Do not forget the afflicted" (Ps 10:12).

"Remember this: the enemy has mocked Yahweh, and a foolish people has insulted Your name. Do not give the life of Your dove to beasts; do not forget the lives of Your poor people forever. Do not forget the clamor of Your adversaries, the tumult of Your opponents that goes up constantly" (Ps 74:18-19,23).

Did you identify? If so with which passage(s) and why?

I remember a time when my dad, my pastor, was being unjustly treated by some church members. Note that not every church member is a Christian, and even those of us who are saved can be misled into making horrible mistakes.

I could really identify with Asaph as I prayed for my folks. During that time, I would have jotted down Psalm 74:23. "God, have you forgotten our enemies? Did you forget how they treat my dad and what they say?"

Because the stress and sadness were so great, it felt like God had forgotten about this one pastor in this one town in this one city in this one state in this one country. It seemed that He didn't even remember him at all. That's how I felt, but is that a fact? You may feel forgotten, but is that feeling the same thing as a fact? Does God truly forget?

> **Look at what Scripture says about God's forgetfulness.**
>
> Deuteronomy 4:31 says God will not forget His _____ because He is _____.
>
> Hebrews 6:10 says God won't forget your _____ and your _____.

God says He will not forget His covenant or our work and labor of love. He didn't "forget" my dad; He will never forget. Notice the Scriptures above.

> **Did God say He "can't" forget or He "won't" forget?**
>
>
> **What importance do you attach to His choice of words?**
>
>
> **What do the words "I will" mean to you?**

"I will" denotes choice and volition. There is nothing God can't do, for He is limitless in power. My friend, God won't forget you. He doesn't forget your pain, frustration, or any detail of your life. He only chooses to forget one thing.

What is it according to Isaiah 43:25 and Hebrews 8:12?

God claims to wipe out and not "remember" our sin. I love that.

What picture represents God's attitude toward remembering our sin in Psalm 103:12?

What significance do you see in the terms "east" and "west"?

I believe God inspired David to use east and west because the north and south poles are a finite distance apart. East and west are an infinite distance apart. You can just keep going east or west forever.

We can't grasp an infinite distance, but this is God we're talking about. If He is infinite, how can our sin be lost to Him? Is your brain in pain?

Here's the best way I can think of this (and, please don't think it irreverent—it's just an analogy): Imagine God as a computer and His "memory" is complete—no data needs to be added and none can be deleted. So, how could God possibly forget? Isn't our sin stored in His memory? Does He press the "delete" key? I am no Bill Gates, but my understanding is that data is not truly deleted from a hard drive though we hit the delete key. Some computer geek still has the skill to find and to retrieve it. In other words, our sin isn't deleted; it is totally retrievable.

The truth is that God *won't* retrieve our forgiven sin, not that He *can't*. God doesn't keep our sin in RAM—random access memory—instead it is archived, never to be retrieved again.

God doesn't call it to mind. He removes it as far as the east is from the west—as far as from your desktop to that bottomless hole in cyber space which swallows up our data like a hungry garbage disposal. It's hidden way deep somewhere in God's vast database, archived deep in the folder of His forgiveness. Because He is so totally dependable, our sin is gone with the certainty as if He had forgotten.

> In Genesis 41:51, Joseph gives a good picture of what it means to forget. It doesn't erase an event; forgetting just means you overlook it. Why do you think Scripture says so much about God remembering?

When Scripture uses the word "remember" it isn't an "Oh yeah, I forgot!" kind of remembering. It denotes attentiveness or regard. For example, in Genesis 30:22 "God remembered Rachel."

God didn't just suddenly remember He created the woman. He showed her regard and attention.

In Exodus 2:24, God "remembered His covenant with Abraham, Isaac, and Jacob." He didn't just say "Oh yeah … how could I have forgotten?" When Scripture says He remembered His covenant; it means He gave heed to, regarded, or acknowledged it.

So, when you consider Hannah or David or whomever you identified with, they are simply asking God, "Regard me, Lord; take heed of my plight."

God is aware of you, knows you, and regards you with value worthy of His attention. God knows you and everything about you, yet chooses not to remember—pay attention to, regard, or heed—our sin. That's not a contradiction; rather it's an example of His amazing grace.

God can disregard our sin because Jesus already dealt with it for us. God regarded it with wrath on Calvary once and for all. The reason your sin is never retrieved from God's memory is because His "screen saver" is a picture of His Son on your cross.

Psalm 32:1-2 describes your position. Rephrase it into a prayer of gratefulness for God's forgetful omniscience.

Dear God,

Amen

Well, we've spent four weeks together and I appreciate you sticking with this! I know not everything makes complete sense, but He makes everything beautiful in His time. So hang in there!

1. Madhavi Acharya-Tom Yew, "IBM supercomputer Watson gets a job on Wall Street after conquering Jeopardy," *The Star* [online], 6 March 2012 [cited 13 April 2012]. Available from the Internet: *www.thestar.com*
2. "Omniscient," *Dictionary.com* [online, cited 13 April 2012]. Available from the Internet: *http://dictionary.reference.com*
3. Don Nori, *The Prayer God Loves to Answer* (Shippensburg, PA: Destiny Image Publishers, 2006), 43.
4. *The Complete C.S. Lewis Signature Classics* (New York: HarperCollins, 2002), 640. Available on the Internet: *http://books.google.com*

Group Session

Video Notes

When we compare ourselves to _____ _____, we can feel _____.

Consider yourself "_____-_____."

God Himself _____ _____ to make you great (see Ps. 18:35).

When you hear your own name, you know that _____ _____ _____.

Conversation Guide

1. Share with the group a time when you felt insignificant. What role did comparison play in that situation?

2. How does the knowledge that you are in-significant change the way you feel about yourself? About God?

3. How should you respond to the truth that you matter to God? That He knows and seeks you?

week five

God, Do You Hear Prayer?

In college I helped lead worship with Paul, the most spiritually mature guy my age I knew. He prayed in a way I had never heard before. He stretched himself across the floor, nose to the ground. I couldn't pray with Paul; he was obviously more connected with God than I was.

In my mind, my posture of crossed legs and hands was not nearly as spiritual or as acceptable to God. I honestly thought, *Does God really hear me pray? Does He only hear people like Paul?* After all, I had some unanswered prayer in my life that supported my questions. When prayers go unanswered, it can rip a big hole in our blanket of faith. We wonder, *Does God really hear every prayer? If He does, why doesn't He always answer?* If you've ever asked those questions, you are in good company.

Jesus tasted unanswered prayer on the cross: "My God, My God, why have You forsaken Me?" (Matt. 27:46). No response came from Heaven for Jesus and often no response comes for us. At Jesus' baptism and transfiguration, God spoke assuring He was attentive and listening. But, during the darkest moments of Christ's earthly life, God answered only with silence and darkness.

Jesus' response to unanswered prayer was commitment, "Father, into Your hands I entrust My spirit" (Luke 23:46). Do you know what He was saying? He was giving us an understanding that we can trust Father God, even with unanswered prayer.

Unanswered prayers may break your heart. They never make sense. But, can you choose to be loyal to God even so? You can if you understand to whom you are committing yourself. God does hear your prayer. In fact, He listens for it. Can you entrust yourself into His hands? This week as you consider this question, will you entrust your missing pieces into God's hands?

Day 1 "Can you hear me? Can you hear me now?!"

"Ring, Ring … Hello … Hello?" Just curious, how many times have you held a cell phone to your ear and asked, "Can you hear me now?" If you're like me, you've done that too many times to count! In fact, so many of us have that experience that Verizon Wireless capitalized on our frustration by featuring actor Paul Marcarelli uttering those very words in their famous cell phone commercials.[1]

It's frustrating to try to connect with someone on the phone and not really know if they hear us, isn't it? When we pray for a long time with no answer, we can feel that same frustration and even wonder if God hears us—"God, can You hear me? Can You hear me now?" The big question isn't *can* God hear us, but rather *does* God hear us?

> **What does the question posed in Psalm 94:9 imply about God's hearing?**

If He can hear, why does it seem like He doesn't hear us? Does He have selective hearing? Maybe the question isn't does God hear, but *what* does He hear?

> **According to Psalm 5:3, God hears _____.**
>
> **God hears your voice. What did He hear from you this morning?**

> **According to Psalm 10:17-18, God hears _____.**
>
> **God hears the desire of those who suffer and gives them strength. When it comes to the missing pieces in your life, what is the desire He hears from you?**

> **According to 1 John 5:14-15, God hears _____.**

God hears when you pray according to His will. What have you prayed lately that is according to His will?

According to Psalm 34:15-17, God hears _____.

The righteous are those who know Him and are known by Him. They aren't pious and perfect; they are simply made righteous by God's grace through faith in Christ. Righteousness is not achieved through our effort; righteousness is received when we receive Christ as Savior.

I know you've been doing this Bible study for about five weeks now, but, please, may I ask you, are you one of "the righteous"? Do you know Him? Do you really know Him or just know about Him? You may have come to church but that isn't the same as coming to the cross and trusting Jesus for forgiveness and relationship with God.

Put simply, have you accepted Christ's gift of grace? If so, jot down when you trusted Christ and how your relationship with Him has grown.

If you can't fill in the above, Girl (or Guy), this is your moment. Call a Bible study buddy or a friend you know is a Christian and tell her. Ask her to guide you to faith in Christ so you can be born again.

God hears His righteous ones. Yet, God still won't hear our prayers under some conditions.

What does Psalm 66:18 say about times God won't listen to our prayers?

What does James 4:3 add to the issue?

Don't make this into a test God grades to see if we pass. God wants to hear our prayers, but because He loves us, He will not reward actions based on malice in our hearts or selfishness in our desires. When we come to God with a pure heart, right motives, and pray according to His will as one of His righteous ones, He hears us.

You'll find no better example of praying with right motives than Jesus Himself. Come and join Him in the garden of Gethsemane.

What did Jesus pray in Mark 14:35?

Before His crucifixion, Jesus prayed that if it were possible, the hour might pass from Him. Now let me ask you a question.

Was it possible? Read Mark 14:36 if you need help with the answer.

Interestingly, you could have answered either way. Jesus knew it was possible because with God all things are possible. Jesus also knew His mission was to give His life as a ransom for us sinners (see Mark 10:45).

Jesus knew the Father's will, yet He asked anyway. What are your thoughts on what Jesus did?

I wonder if Jesus posed that prayer as much for our sakes as His. As a man He certainly longed for another way. He wanted the cup of suffering to pass even though He knew it was His to drink. Perhaps, just as He taught us through the last supper, He showed us how we can pray to our Father with honest abandon. We can appeal to Him about anything because with Him all things are possible and He hears us. But, perhaps Jesus also posed that prayer so we could see the difference between what is possible and what is best.

The hour could have passed from Him. The results would have been convenient for Him, but they would have been eternally disastrous for us.

Do you pray for what is possible or what is best? When you pray with unselfish motives and a pure heart focused on His will, you pray for what is best, not merely what is possible.

Read the final phrase of Mark 14:36. How did Jesus end His prayer?

Jesus concluded with "not what I will, but what You will." God hears requests for His will. Jesus prayed for God's will instead of His own will.

Whose will do you pray for most of the time? Be honest.

> ## My friend, God cares about you. He cares enough to hear; He cares enough to answer—even when that answer is not what you want or expect.

Are you willing to pray like Jesus? Are you willing to appeal to God's power yet yield to His will? Finish up today by expressing your thoughts concerning praying for God's will by writing a prayer psalm below. You don't need to make it poetic, just honest.

Read Psalm 5:1-4,7-8,11-12 to give you inspiration or as a guide in writing your prayer psalm.

Lord, hear my prayer. Amen.

A piece of praise from David:

"May God be praised! He has not turned away my prayer or turned His faithful love from me." *Psalm 66:20*

Day 2 Eloquent Silence

Shhh … let's start our time today with silence. Pause and quiet your soul, your phone, your TV, or whatever noise is going on around you. In my case, I'll give my dog Lucy a bone so she won't whine.

Now, pause and sit quietly for a few moments. Stillness …

How do you feel after sitting silently for a while?

The way I feel about silence depends on what is going on in my life or heart. Sometimes silence is relaxing; it brings tranquility. Other times, it can make me way too aware of my anxiety, stress, or anything else I would rather avoid. So sometimes silence makes me want to avoid silence.

Are you ever uncomfortable with silence? When you are alone, do you need a radio or TV on just to fill the emptiness? If so, why do you think you dislike silence?

How about silence from a person? When a person is silent, what kind of thoughts or emotions do you have in response?

○ nervous   ○ hurt   ○ indifferent
○ offended   ○ sad   ○ isolated
○ paranoid   ○ curious

What do you think people's silence often represents?

○ rudeness   ○ aloofness   ○ disinterest
○ insensitivity ○ apathy   ○ tiredness
○ punishment   ○ judgment   ○ insecurity

The way we feel about human silence results from how we perceive the motives of another's silence. If we feel someone is simply being rude and that's why they are silent, we may feel offended or hurt. If we believe someone's silence is judgmental, our response may be nervousness. We need to think about this because we often lump God and His silence in with all the tangled feelings we have about human silence.

When it comes to God, how do you tend to feel when He is silent?

If you've prayed and heard nothing from Him, what do you think His silence often represents?

Were the answers to the last two questions similar to the answers you gave to the two questions that preceded them? What does that suggest to you?

Do you have the same response to God's silence as you do to human silence? If you do, stop and ask God to remind you that He is not I feel or I assume. He is a just, compassionate, ever-present God whose motives and ways are perfect—He is I Am.

We aren't the only ones who have felt uneasy about God's silence. Read the following verses and describe in your own words with what each writer equates God's silence.

The composer of Psalm 35:22 seems to think if God is silent, He is also

_____.

We often equate God's silence with Him being distant. Have you ever felt far from God because He was silent? Tell me about it please.

Were you actually far from Him or was He there all along? Silence can make you feel far from God, but every feeling is not a fact. He is Immanuel; God with you.

What do you think the writer in Psalm 39:12 thought God's silence represented?

He seemed to me to equate God's silence with loneliness or rejection. He didn't consider himself a citizen but an alien.

Have you ever felt as if you didn't belong due to God's silence? If so, how did it feel?

How does Philippians 3:20 reassure you that you are not alienated from God because He is silent?

Silence can make you feel rejected. Every feeling is not a fact though. Remember you are accepted in the Beloved and He will never leave you or forsake you.

What did Asaph consider silence to equal in Psalm 83:1?

Asaph equated silence with stillness or inactivity. Have you ever felt like God was simply not active on your behalf because He was silent?

Friend, don't lose hope if God is silent. He's not sleeping or inactive, even if it feels that way. You may be familiar with this statement by now: "Every feeling is not a _____." That's right; every feeling is not a fact. The truth is He never sleeps or slumbers; He is always moving on your behalf.

Isaiah states another aspect of God's silence. In Isaiah 64:12 he asks, "Lord, after all this, will You restrain Yourself? Will You keep silent and afflict severely?" Sometimes God's silence feels like He is holding Himself at a distance or even punishing us. When He holds back or remains quiet, it hurts.

Have you felt hurt or punished by God's silence? If so, describe.

I know that's not easy to feel. I also know, however, that God is kind. While He may hold back His hand, He will never withhold from you His heart.

When God is silent we can feel He is distant. As a result we feel lonely. We can feel God is inactive or showing unnecessary restraint that hurts us. Since every feeling isn't a fact, however, perhaps God's silence could be an act of love.

One Friday, Connor came home from second grade and instructed, "Mom, get out your laptop so I can work on Microsoft Word!"

I complied with the 7-year-old Bill Gates and started up Baby Dell. I should tell you I named my laptop. Ask anyone in an airport with me; I always take Baby Dell out of his bag as I go through security and introduce him to the TSA agents who handle him with care. I'm sure they think I'm a little loony, but no one messes with my computer!

I placed Baby Dell on Connor's lap and heard Connor pecking at the keys. "Mom, don't listen." He asserted. "I am writing you a letter."

I told him I wasn't, but, it's really hard for a mother to ignore her child and a blind woman not to hear—especially when Baby Dell talks. (When Baby Dell talks, Mama Jenn listens.)

I heard Connor spelling, "Dear Mom, I lo …" He was trying to type "love," but when he couldn't find the "V" he paused and grunted.

I silently cheered him on; "Come on Connor! It's right by the C!" because I knew for Connor, he needed to find the "V" by himself.

After a minute, I heard it! "V" followed by "E" and soon the document was complete. He proudly read it to me and I cheered aloud.

I could have easily typed the "V" for him, but I remained silent. Why do you think I did that?

When do you think silence is a loving response to another's frustration?

It is most kind for a parent to give her child a chance to try, even if they fail, and afford opportunity for growth and success. I may have been silent, but I was totally supportive.

> Sometimes God is silent when we are struggling the most. God could easily rescue us when we get stuck also, but would it be the kindest act? Why or Why not?

Because of His goodness, God sometimes allows us to endure His silence and feel frustration. If He quickly threw out answers or stepped in and rescued us, what would we learn? How could we grow?

Don't be discouraged when you feel stuck. Don't think God is disengaged just because He's silent.

> So, here's a question for you; what is your "V" that you just can't find? What is that missing piece when it comes to prayer that you are looking for and wish God would just point it out or provide?

> What promise does God give in Psalm 138:8?

> He reassures He is listening and active even though He may be silent. How does this verse encourage you?

God's silence is always compassionate and never cruel. If you have had a relationship with someone who seeks to punish or control with their silence, it can be easy to assume God's silence is the same. It is not. Because God is good, His silence is a reflection of His good purposes. His silence stems from Him being good and seeking to accomplish good in and for you.

So, my friend, relax in His silence. Don't try to fill it with lesser voices or useless noise. Trust He is offering you silent support.

Day 3 It's Your Move God

My little brother David isn't so little anymore! It shouldn't surprise me he grew up to be a lawyer. He could always outthink me. When we were kids, we lived in a tiny house in Miami, Florida. It didn't seem tiny until I grew up and realized all five of us humans and one dog were crammed into one thousand square feet.

The best feature of our home was the pool in the backyard. The previous owners custom built it with a tile chessboard about a foot under water. It was dotted with sand-filled, waterproof, stout chessmen each standing about 6 inches tall. A few of the pieces had served as the dog's chew toys, but other than that, it was an excellent playing opportunity, so I learned chess!

My most vivid memories were playing against David. He was almost 10 years younger than I, and he always beat me—or I would just give up before he had a chance to! I approached chess like a relay race, and he approached it like a marathon. He took his time, studied the board, and thought about strategy while his big sister just moved the first piece she touched. I would impatiently tell him to hurry up, but he'd just sit there as if he wasn't listening to me at all. We had fun, and if I quit the game before his strategy unfolded, we would simply toss the pawns in the deep end and dive after them. David was slow to move and would think ahead. I wanted to win, was impulsive, and was all about the next move. He was about the whole board.

God sees the whole board, not just the next move. His knowledge is vast, long, deep, and often invisible to us. We want to measure if He is listening to our prayers by the movement on the board, and often all we get is silence and stillness. Isaiah 64 expresses well the way we often feel when we just want to see something from God so we know He is listening.

What did Isaiah long for God to do in 64:1?

Now, if suddenly the sky ripped open, the mountains quaked, and God came down, Isaiah would know God heard and listened to him, wouldn't he?! Think about it: Is instant response the way you know God is listening to you? Do you grow impatient on this side of the chessboard waiting for a move?

Sometimes we feel just like Isaiah. "Oh, that You would make this house sell. … Oh that You would heal the cancer …" We know how that feels, don't we? I wonder if that's how Habakkuk felt also?

Habakkuk, the eighth of the Minor Prophets, prayed about the unjust behavior of his people.

What did he pray in Habakkuk 1:2? Express the idea in your own words.

Habakkuk associated long-prayed, unanswered prayers with God simply not listening. When we pray "how long" prayers, we can wonder if God is listening to us too.

I felt that way when blindness met menopause! The result was depression. It lasted far longer than I expected. I remember praying the "how long" prayer. "How long Lord will I be in this low place, with no energy and ability to do life?" When we pray a Habakkuk-like "how long" prayer, it is often followed by an Isaiah-like "oh, that You would" prayer. For me, it was "Oh that You would just heal me, lift me, and pull me out of this pit!"

What is your "how long" prayer?

What is your "oh, that You would" prayer?

Has God answered those prayers? Do you think He is listening? Did God listen to Habakkuk's prayers for justice?

Read Habakkuk 1:5. God not only listened, He answered. What did God say?

God told Habakkuk He was going to answer his prayer and that Habakkuk was going to be utterly amazed. Isn't that just like God? While we are crying out "how long" and "oh, that You would" prayers, wondering if He is even listening, God is already in process of answering our prayers! We find ourselves impatiently waiting for the next move to indicate God is in the game, when He is actually busy moving His plan along without a single pawn leaving its square.

Can you relate? What prayers have you prayed that God answered in a greatly unexpected way?

If God spoke to you as He did Habakkuk and said you would be amazed about what He is "going to do," what would you expect that outcome to be?
○ great   ○ hopeful   ○ other:
○ exciting   ○ disappointing
○ appropriate   ○ painful

Hold that thought and put a star by your response because tomorrow we will revisit it and dive deeper into God's answer. Now, take some time and think about it. What do you expect when God says you will be amazed by what He is going to do? What do you do in the mean time?

What did Habakkuk do while he waited for God to move in Habakkuk 2:1?
○ He prayed more.
○ He worried.
○ He waited and watched.

Having closed his appeal to Yahweh, the prophet took his stand on the watchtower to look and listen for what God would do and say.

When you're awaiting an answer from God, what best describes your posture?

○ on my knees
○ wringing my hands
○ looking from the watchtower
○ falling into a pit of despair

○ shaking an angry fist
○ rolling my eyes in annoyance
○ looking at my watch
○ other:

Use Matthew 24:42 and Ephesians 6:18 as a guide to write a prayer expressing your desire to wait well for God's answer.

Dear God,

Amen

Habakkuk sat patiently on this side of the chessboard watching, waiting, and knowing God would move visibly how and when He chose and that His move would always be right.

Let's do the same, OK?

Today, meditate upon this piece of truth:

"From ancient times no one has heard, no one has listened, no eye has seen any God except You, who acts on behalf of the one who waits for Him." *Isaiah 64:4*

Day 4 Snakes & Rocks vs. Fish & Bread

We haven't shared a cup of coffee lately, so why don't you pour yourself a cup and sip slowly while we spend time together today? Yesterday, I asked you to put a star by what you expect from God when He tells you He is going to amaze you with His answer to your prayer (p. 115).

What did you check as your response?

Why did you choose that response?

If God told me He was about to amaze me, I would be brimming with excitement and anticipation. Yeehaw! I'd be quoting "Every generous act and every perfect gift is from above" (Jas. 1:17) and smiling big about God because He is good and gives good gifts. Often when God gives us a clue we will be amazed by His answer, it feels like anticipating a Christmas present or a surprise party. When God told Habakkuk he would be amazed, it was a surprise coming alright, but no party included.

Turn back to Habakkuk 1:6-11, where we ended up yesterday. What was the surprise nature of God's answer to Habakkuk's prayer?

How did God describe the Chaldeans (or Babylonians)?

OK, so they weren't the nicest of people. God captures the nature of this enemy with words like "bitter," "impetuous," "fierce," and "terrifying," just to name a few. I'd say that's the kind of amazing answer to prayer we wouldn't want.

Habakkuk longed for the injustice of his people to cease. He pleaded with God to help them live rightly. But, perhaps Habakkuk and God had different answers in mind. Couldn't God just rain down some manna as a reminder of His goodness and that kindness would lead them to repent? That would amaze, wouldn't it? But, the amazing answer was in the form of an enemy attack.

Sister, not every answer we receive is a good one from our perspective.

> **How do you usually respond when you get bad answers to your requests from God?**

We expect God to give us what is good in response to our prayer. And, there's biblical support for that expectation. Read Matthew 7:9.

> **To whom does Jesus compare God in this verse?**
> ○ king   ○ genie
> ○ father   ○ benefactor
> ○ pushover

> **What two comparisons does Jesus make contrasting "good" gifts with "bad" ones in Matthew 7:9-10?**

> **What does that tell you about God's character and His response to our requests?**

Our Father God is good and doesn't do a bait and switch—we don't ask Him for daily bread just so He will give us pebbles and boulders. Still, it doesn't always feel like His answers are good ones. What are we to do when we experience bad answers? If God promises to give us what is good, then why do we end up with what we feel like is a snake?

When Habakkuk prayed, the Chaldeans must have felt like a snakey answer rather than the fishy response he hoped for. What a hard provision.

Why do we get bad answers? Or are they really bad? Hmm … Think about it.

How could what you think is bad really be good from another perspective?

Consider this, and pour another cup of coffee if you're a fast drinker like me. I thought God handed me a bunch of rocks and a snake when Phil and I moved to a new community and a new church. I had a couple of CDs I had recorded and had been traveling leading worship and sharing concerts. The new church knew this, yet they never asked me to sing. I grew more curious and frustrated as the months turned into a year. I prayed, wondering why God wasn't opening that door; after all, that was my gift and my ministry.

At the same time, Phil was asked to teach a college Bible study and asked me to team teach with him. I had never taught before. I found the experience challenging, and each week I taught, it revealed a gift I didn't know I had. The more I taught, the more passionate I became about teaching. God graciously rejected my plea to share in the music ministry because He wanted to give me time to grow in teaching. What I thought was a snakey answer was really a fish in disguise.

Snakes and scorpions bite, sting, and hurt. When we live with the painful answer to our prayers, we assume they are snakes and scorpions because it hurts; the answer stings. When we look back, we see they were fish and bread in disguise because they nourished and grew us. It may seem like a snake at the time, but when you look back, you may see it was the fish God promised because He is a Father who only gives good gifts.

Can you think of any snakes or rocks you thought you received that turned out to be fish and bread? If so, explain.

What was given and multiplied in Matthew 14:15-21?

Consider this: God will not give snakes and rocks to us because they hurt. What He gives to us, He grants so we can also give. Look at Matthew 14:19.

What was the progression of the fish and bread? Who got it and who gave it to whom?

The fish and bread God gives to us in response to our prayers is the fish and bread He wants us to give to others. He provides for us, nourishes, and grows us, and in turn, we give from the abundance we have received. So, even if it feels like snakes and stones, treat it like the fish and bread it is!

God always answers with what is best even if it isn't what we consider "good." We quantify good not based on the quality of the answer, but on the quality of the character of the One who gives the answer. In other words, since God is good, His answer is always best.

A piece of encouragement:
" 'We only have five loaves and two fish here,' they said to Him. 'Bring them here to Me,' He said. ... Everyone ate and was filled." *Matthew 14:17-20*

Day 5 The Ultimate Answer

"I really don't think God plays favorites when it comes to football," the cranky guy snorted from the bleacher in front of us. At least he waited for Andrea to say the "amen" of her prayer before his big doctrinal pronouncement. "I know," Andrea apologetically conceded, "We just can't afford to lose this game!" I listened quietly sitting beside her as she and Reverend Cranky had a brief theological discussion about prayer.

A bunch of us middle-aged moms had gathered to watch our friends' son play football. We happened to be sitting on the home team side, and we were the visitors. I guess that's why Mr. Cranky felt if we were going to appeal to God for a win, it should at least be for his team.

Does God really hear those kinds of prayers? And, if He does, then does He respond with an answer—you know, like if enough people pray for the red team, God will say, "OK, the red team wins"? Now, before you think I am Reverend Cranky's evil twin, let me share this. When I was a college student, a well-known Christian singer came to our university to perform. His music was totally inspiring and engaging. After a few songs, he shared how he'd noticed that Christian Dance Clubs were beginning to pop up around the country. Of course, all the college students erupted in applause and "whoop" filled the arena.

We were abruptly stopped as the singer interrupted our cheer with "Don't you know there are people dying and going to hell, children starving, and Christians are dancing?" It took a moment for us to realize he was serious and seriously miffed at our clapping. He then proceeded to scold and shame us for even considering the notion of dancing when people are suffering. The rest of the concert felt more like being grounded or sent to our rooms.

I felt like a Christian brother slapped our hands, sucked the joy out of our faith, and rained judgment down on us all. That is not what I want you to experience as we think about this subject—especially if you've prayed for a football win or an empty parking spot before.

Andrea's heart was pure when she appealed to God for her football win. God heard her, and I bet He even smiled. I'm not condemning the content of anyone's prayer. I just want us to think about what God hears when we pray.

Yesterday we considered how God does hear and answer our prayers. Turn back to Matthew 7, and let's see what else Jesus says about prayer.

> What three verbs does Jesus tell us in Matthew 7:7 to employ when we pray?
> 1.
> 2.
> 3.
>
> And, what are the results listed in verse 8?
> 1.
> 2.
> 3.

We ask, seek, and knock then receive, find, and experience an open door. Does that mean we can ask, seek, and knock about even football games? Hmm … Isn't a football win sort of like asking for bread or fish? You remember from yesterday, Jesus compared God to a good father who gives bread when it's requested, not a stone or snake.

> How did Jesus conclude the Father/God comparison in Matthew 7:11? If earthly fathers, who are _____, give _____ to their children, how much more will your Heavenly Father give _____to_____.

The Greek word at the end of the verse translated "good" (agatha) is a plural noun form and refers to the plural "good gifts" in the phrase that comes right before it.[2] More than one good gift is acknowledged; God promises to give us good gifts. What could those possibly be? Football wins?

> What do you think "good gifts" means?

If you look at the context of Jesus' words in Matthew 6–7, you'll find good gifts connected to developing your character. God's good gifts lead to you and me giving, praying, forgiving, fasting, storing up treasure, not worrying, eating, and being wise.

If you were discipling a new believer, how would you explain that those fruits of a godly character may be some of the good gifts God is concerned about giving us?

Perhaps the good gifts Jesus refers to are spiritual or at least some of the best of them are. Giving, not worrying, fasting, and praying are all good things that if we ask, we will be given; if we seek those good things, we will find them; if we knock on their doors, those doors will be open to us so we can obey Christ's commands and walk fruitfully. These good things are gifts from our Father in Heaven.

That doesn't mean that God only answers prayers concerning spiritual things, but it does make me pay attention to what I'm praying. Is it with a pure heart? Is it according to His will? If you want to dive deeper into this, I challenge you to read Paul's letters in the New Testament. See what he mentions he prays for and see what he asks others to pray. It just may transform your prayers—it has mine.

Anyway, back to the good gifts. The good gifts Matthew described broadly, Luke pinpoints.

What is the good gift according to Luke 11:13?

The ultimate of the good gifts God will give to those who ask is the gift of the Holy Spirit —the gift of God Himself.

Read John 14:16-18,26. What characteristics of the Holy Spirit reveal why He is the ultimate answer?

The Holy Spirit is *the Good Gift, the* ultimate response because His presence is more comforting and satisfying than any other answer you could receive from God. He is our Comforter, our Helper, and the One who teaches and guides us into truth. He is our Companion. I think Habakkuk may have really understood that. God gave him answers that were hard to hear. But, read Habakkuk 3:17-19.

Does Habakkuk sound disappointed or satisfied? Why?

My friend, the reason Habakkuk was satisfied— the reason you can be satisfied no matter the answer you receive—is because God gives the Good Gift to each of us. Satisfaction doesn't come from answers to your prayer. Satisfaction comes from the encounter you have with God through His Spirit because of your prayer. Answers never fully satisfy—only relationship with God satisfies.

You will lose hope if you wait for answers to fill in your missing pieces. The only hope that is real and lasting is the hope that comes from Christ Himself.

God's ultimate answer to our prayers is the good gift of the Holy Spirit. He is the affirmation that God is with us. Because of the Holy Spirit, we know God listens to us, hears our concerns, and answers well.

So, do you think I am Mrs. Cranky? I hope not. I love you and want you to not settle for lesser gifts and smaller answers when it comes to prayer.

Oh, and P.S. Our football team lost! Score one for Mr. Cranky and his boys.

Girl, week 5 is a wrap. "God, do You hear our prayers?" I hope you know the answer to be a huge *yes*. Since He does hear, I want you to know He hears me pray for you as you complete this study. I pray His Spirit plants seeds of truth in you that blossom into a huge crop that nourishes you and others!

Peace to you my friend.

A piece of truth from Paul:

"In the same way the Spirit also joins to help in our weakness, because we do not know what to pray for as we should, but the Spirit Himself intercedes for us with unspoken groanings. And He who searches the hearts knows the Spirit's mind-set, because He intercedes for the saints according to the will of God." *Romans 8:26-27*

1. Mark Cina, "Verizon disconnects Can You Hear Me Now?" *Hollywood Reporter* [online], 14 April 2011 [cited 13 April 2012]. Available from the Internet: *www.reuters.com*
2. "Agatha," *Englishman's Greek Concordance* [onilne, cited 13 April 2012]. Available from the Internet: *www.concordances.org*

Group Session

Video Notes

Different responses to unanswered prayer:

Angie _____

Bonnie _____

Connie _____

Matilda _____

Vicky _____

When we pray, we:

_____ God's power.

_____ to His will.

Conversation Guide

1. How do you typically respond to unanswered prayer?

2. What's the difference between appealing to God's power and appealing to His will?

3. Consider a situation in which you've repeatedly asked the Lord for help or healing. How can you demonstrate to Him that you will trust His heart toward you in that instance—even if you can't see Him intervening?

week six

God, Do You Err?

Do you have an *I* in your name? Jennifer does! Sarah used to …

In Genesis 17:15, Abraham's wife Sarah's name was changed. She was originally named Sarai. And, believe me, while her name was Sarai, she had a big letter *I* in it.

God had promised that she would bear a child, but His plan didn't unfold in Sarai's perfect timing. So, since she thought God may have erred, she took matters into her own hands. She basically said: *I* have a promise (see Gen. 15:4-5; 17:16). *I* have born no children, but *I* have a slave (see Gen. 16:1). She told Abram, since God has kept me from having a child, since obviously, God's ways aren't perfect, *I* will give you Hagar and maybe *I* will build a family through her (see Gen. 16:2). Let me Summarize for Sarai: *I* know better than God. My way is perfect, not His.

Because Sarai had a big letter *I*, she did not rest in God's plan, rather she resisted it. Did you notice *resist* has a big *I* in it? And, so does *sin* and *pride*. When we have a big letter *I*, we resist God's perfect plan. "*I* want my way; *I* know best; *I* think my plan is perfect …"

God's way is perfect because He does not err even when we do. In Genesis 21:1 God came to Sarah as He said and did as He promised. In verse 2, Sarah became pregnant and bore a son … at God's appointed time.

As Job said, "I know that You can do anything and no plan of Yours can be thwarted" (42:2). God always accomplishes His perfect plan. There are no missing pieces in His plan because He does not err.

Day 1 Perfectly Strange; Strangely Perfect!

My first boyfriend was named Isaiah. No, he wasn't the Old Testament prophet; his last name was Alvarez. He was the cute, blue-eyed Cuban boy from Miami who sat behind me at church. He was debonair and charming, and much to my pleasure, he was a year older than me—17. He pronounced my name, "Yen-neefer," and as far as I was concerned, he was "muy guapo" and his suave accent was the brogue of the divine. I loved everything the teenage Don Juan did and uttered. He said all the right things; he was polite and always a gentleman; he treated my parents with respect and kept me charmed and entertained. I spent hours dreaming about him and writing his name over and over. I have quite a few pages of my diary dedicated to all Isaiah's amazing virtues! I thought he was astonishingly, absolutely fabulous … I thought he was perfect.

That is, until we went out on our first date. It wasn't a disaster; it was just a big dose of reality—he was a great guy, but like me, very far from perfect. Our puppy love affair whimpered away within weeks.

We often think people are perfect before we get to know them intimately, don't we? But, the opposite is true of God. We may think from a distance, *He can't be perfect; look at what He allows.* Upon getting to know Him better, our opinion may change.

> **What is your opinion about Him? Does He seem "perfect" to you? Are His ways "perfect"?**

We may concede He is perfect, but His ways don't always seem so. A prayer by Walter Brueggemann captures many people's feelings about God and His ways.

> We would as soon you were stable and reliable.
> We would as soon you were predictable
>   and always the same toward us.
> We would like to take the hammer of doctrine
>   and take the nails of piety

and nail your feet to the floor
and have you stay in one place.
And then we find you moving,
always surprising us,
always coming at us from new directions.
Always planting us
and uprooting us
and tearing all things down
and making all things new.[1]

Those lines beautifully express how God's ways aren't always what we expect. Often our perception of His character confuses us. If we were to create what we think is our "ideal" God, it wouldn't be as mysterious as Yahweh. Ours would be perfect according to our standards. When God doesn't behave like we expect or prefer, we can think His ways are flawed. Is He really beyond error?

Let's pretend for just a moment that we don't know the one true God, our precious Father God—Yahweh. Instead, create a want ad describing your ideal God—a being perfect in power and perfect in His ways.

Describe the attributes your ideal God would possess.

Mine would read: "Wanted: a God who does whatever I want and is smarter than me; one who always consoles me and gives me great advice; one who never disagrees with me; one who either overlooks my selfishness or laughs at my sin and negotiates the standards with me; one who keeps me safe and a God who sticks with me no matter what and makes my life peaceful. Oh and I want a God who obliterates all the calories from dark chocolate!"

Creating a God according to our own standards is a dangerous thing none of us would actually seek to do. Yet, sometimes the reason we are confused about

God's ways is because deep down, we think He should be a certain way. After all, that would be perfect, wouldn't it? God's ways can be strange, or are they strangely perfect? Hmm …

That we think rightly about God and His character is essential. Read what God said to Eliphaz in Job 42:7.

> Why was God angry at Eliphaz and his two friends?

God takes seriously how we perceive and proclaim His character. Let's see a few verses that extol the perfect nature of God.

> What does Deuteronomy 32:4 tell you about God's works and ways?

> What does 2 Samuel 7:22 add about God's nature?

> How does the psalmist describe God in Psalm 145:3?

What an expression of God's greatness. The psalmist writes that we cannot even know how great He is. Using some of the Scriptures and adjectives above, create a want ad for God. Make His ad express His character according to Scripture.

> Write your want ad so as to describe who He is. For some extra help, take a look at these verses too: Psalm 18:30; 86:8; 145:3, Proverbs 5:21; Jeremiah 23:23; 32:17.

WANTED:

Compare the two want ads. Are there differences between the pretend God of your first ad and the one true God depicted in the second want ad?

What did you notice?

We sometimes want a God made in our image. Yet, God calls us to be conformed into His image. Which do you think will bring you more satisfaction? God becoming more like you or you becoming more like the one true God as seen in Jesus Christ?

Jot down your thoughts and call a Bible study buddy to discuss this with her.

If we do not rightly assess God's perfect character, then we can slip into thinking He should be the God of our want ad.

How does Exodus 20:3-7 encourage you to keep God preeminent?

Any sort of misperception we have of God is simply our construction of a graven image—a god made in our image. Our false ideas about God become idols.

God takes seriously how we handle being His name-bearers. If we take His name in vain we exploit and disregard it. And, Sister, many of us assume that only applies to using profanity. Taking His name in vain is far more than that.

What ways can you think of that we take His name in vain?

Taking God's name in vain can be to pray without thought, show disrespect to God's house or people, to be flippant or thoughtless during worship, to not treat God as holy but rather as a BFF in Heaven who you can joke with and about. These are all ways we take His name in vain without even realizing it.

It is easy to understand why we have the tendency to do such things when we realize what our want ad says.

Oh, God, protect us from ourselves! We are flawed in our thinking and so selfish that we often can't see You clearly. We filter everything through the lens of ourselves, our needs, our desires, and our ignorance.

> Rephrase Psalm 18:30 as a prayer to your Heavenly Father. Replace the pronouns (He and His) with You and Yours.

Dear God,

As for You ...

Amen

A piece of insight from C.S. Lewis:

"As long as you are proud you cannot know God. A proud man is always looking down on things and people: and, of course, as long as you are looking down, you cannot see something that is above you."[2]

Day 2 Can the Immutable change?

Let's start the day's study by taking a quiz together.

> When is the last time you changed your hairstyle?
> Have you eaten the same meal for lunch every day for the past month?
> When did you last change purses?
> When you eat out, do you only go to one restaurant?
> When did you last rearrange your furniture?
>
> **What do the above answers indicate about your willingness and ability to change?**

My friend Tammer's (not a typo, her name is Tammer like a hammer) husband is one of the most nonchanging people I know. For example, Don has had the same job at the same company, doing the same thing for 24 years. He's driven the same truck for a decade. In fact, when he wrecked his truck, he replaced it with the exact same truck—the same color and even the same year. He has eaten plain noodles since childhood—no sauces ever. He eats salads with no dressing; he never has and I'm sure he never will!

He actually wears the same clothes he's worn since his 20s—and he's now pushing 50! The same styles, same colors … if one garment gets a hole in it, he replaces it with the exact same one. That's not that hard when all he wears is jeans and golf shirts. Thank goodness he's not still in bell-bottoms. But if the denim company deviates from their normal manufacturing process, woe be unto them, Don is no longer a customer. The painstaking process of finding new jeans he can wear for 30 years makes his blood pressure soar.

He has never used any tool but Craftsman® from Sears®. He says they are durable and if they break, he gets a new one—the exact one. He loves the old-time Christian singers like George Beverly Shea; it's not that the new ones aren't good, it's just that he is happy with the ones he's listened to since 1972. Why change? When I call Tammer, I ask her "How's Don?" and her answer is "The same." And no doubt, she really means it. He is the same; yesterday, today, and, I bet, tomorrow too. But, even Don changes; we all do. The quiz above reveals you change from time to time. In other words, you are *mutable*.

Write some synonyms for mutable. Use a dictionary or thesaurus if needed.

To be "mutable" is to be changeable, variable, inconsistent, fluctuating, or alterable. That definition right there is my testimony—I change *a lot*. When it comes to food, fashion, home décor, and even my spiritual life, I'm the queen of mutable. Do we share that throne? All of us humans are prone to change, but God claims He is not.

At the very beginning of the nation of Israel, Numbers 23 contains the story of Balaam and Balak. The latter was king of Moab. He hired Balaam to curse Israel, but the results were less than satisfactory to Balak.

What did God say about Himself in Numbers 23:19-21?

The first thing God tells Balak is that He doesn't change or lie. What God says, He does. God does not change His Word. Many centuries later, the prophet Malachi reminds Israel that the only reason they haven't been destroyed is the constancy of God (see Mal. 3:6). He stays true to His holy and merciful character no matter what.

In the New Testament we see applied to our lives the principles applied to Israel in the Old Testament. Read Romans 11:28-36.

What did God say about our gifts and callings in Romans 11:29?

God's calling and gifts are irrevocable. That means, once you have it, God won't take it back. His choices do not change. God does not change His Word, standards, or choices.

How does James 1:17 sum up God's immutability?

In our experience every light flickers. Even the brightest arc lamp beams are subject to shadow. Not so with our God. No variableness or shadow of turning affects Him. God is constant and unchanging. Why am I making such an issue of this characteristic of God? Why does it matter if God changes every once in a while? Can't that be OK since you trust Him and know He cares about you?

It matters that God is immutable because if He could change, He would not be perfect. If He weren't perfect, then He would be like us. How can we really trust a God like us? Here's what I mean: if Mr. Cranky's football teams, who you met at the football game in week 5, had a perfect record and it changed, it would mean the team lost a football game, thus changing their record. If something "perfect" changes, it can only change negatively.

So, if a perfect God changes, what does He become? If God changed through some type of modification He would be less—imperfect and incomplete. But the Bible is full of references that point to God's perfect character. One of the most powerful is the word *holy*. I just looked up a few and stated the key ideas like this.
- God calls Himself holy (see Lev. 19:2).
- He says none is holy like God (see 1 Sam. 2:2).
- God, who inhabits praise, is holy (see Ps. 22:3).
- The holy God will show Himself holy in righteousness (see Isa. 5:16).

The original Hebrew word from which we get our word *holy* is *kadash* which means *to hallow, to set apart, sanctify*.[3] It's interesting to me that as our English language has evolved, *holy* has been a beautiful picture of what it means to be set apart. The English word *holy* dates back to about the 11th century with the Old English word, *hālig*. It's an adjective derived from *hāl* meaning "whole." It was used to convey concepts like "uninjured, entire or complete."[4]

I love that because God is holy, He is complete! Could complete change to become more complete? No. If *complete* changed, it would have to change for the worse becoming *incomplete*. God is holy and perfect. He is complete and unchanging. Because He is perfect, holy, and immutable, my friend, you can trust Him. Even if you don't understand His ways, you can trust His character.

A piece of truth from Isaiah (not my boyfriend—this time the prophet!):

"I live in a high and holy place, and with the oppressed and lowly of spirit, to revive the spirit of the lowly and revive the heart of the oppressed." *Isaiah 57:15*

Day 3 Does God Regret?

OK Girl, we are diving straight into the deep end! Yesterday we looked at God's immutability. He doesn't change His will or Word. But does He change His ways, and does He change His mind?

What do you think?

The reason I ask is because several places in Scripture say God expressed regret. How can a perfect, immutable God regret? You may want to pour some strong coffee. This could get a little challenging.

What does the Bible say in Genesis 6:5-8 about the people and the condition of their hearts?

In verse 7, what was God's response to the people's wickedness and evil intentions?

Whoa. How can a perfect, immutable God regret His own action? Let's look at the original Hebrew for a little clarity. The Hebrew word that expresses God's regret is *nacham* and it means *to repent* or *feel regret*.[5] When this word is used referring to God, it doesn't carry the idea of sin, rather it communicates an emotion you and I can understand.

Do you remember in week 4 when we talked about anthropomorphisms? Turn back to page 84 to refresh your memory if you need to. To say God has hands, eyes, or any other human physical characteristic is to use an anthropomorphism, right? Ascribing human feelings to God is called an anthropopathism. Let's examine some Scripture to get a feel for some anthropopathisms.

What does God express feeling in Isaiah 43:24?

Can you relate? When have you ever felt like that?

What does Ezekiel 6:9 portray God feeling?

Have you ever felt hurt and wounded by someone's unfaithfulness?
How did it feel?

What emotion does God express in Psalm 95:10?

What causes you to feel resentment or grief?

All the emotions you read about God are emotions you have felt, right? You've felt weighted down, wounded by others' unfaithfulness, or grieved by the choices of the people you love? Of course you have; we all have. That's the point. Understanding our own feelings provides our best way to understand God's responses. God is perfect, immutable, but His unchanging nature does not mean static or nonfeeling. God is not a supernatural, emotionally flatlined, Mr. Spock! He responds to us with what we recognize as emotion.

So, how does this apply to "regretting" or "repenting"? Think of it this way: Imagine giving a beautiful piece of lace from your grandmother's wedding dress to a 12-year-old girl. When you saw her wiping off her make-up with it, you would respond with grief and hurt. You would regret or repent giving her such a special gift. I think that is what God expresses in Genesis 6.

God, as a Father, feels grieved to the heart, regretful for giving His people a gift. Just as you would feel hurt and have a response to being offended, abused, or neglected, God too has response. The only language we have to describe His response is by using anthropopathisms. God resented man's wickedness. He felt anger because their sin was an insult to His holiness. He was grieved for their sinful choices were an affront to His gracious, merciful heart.

As my editor says, we can unthinkingly accept the human idea that God fits our concept of perfection—beyond feeling emotions. That man-made idea would make God less rather than more. Beware of reducing God in the name of elevating Him. That's not all. Pour yourself more coffee and we'll continue. The people in Noah's day did not repent but the people in Jonah's day did.

What was God's response to Nineveh's repentance in Jonah 3:10?
○ God annihilated them anyway.
○ God relented of His plan and didn't send disaster.

Jonah wasn't happy and told God in no uncertain terms that He shouldn't show mercy to a heathen people. Heedless of the prophet's complaint, God relented anyway. When you read both Noah's account and Jonah's account, it can make you wonder how God can be immutable if He regrets and repents. Since it appears from the Scriptures God has changed His mind should we conclude God is not immutable?

Let's see how those two accounts are compatible with God's immutability rather than contrary to it by considering the following questions.

Did God change His will or standards in the story of Noah's flood?

What is God's will and standard according to 2 Peter 3:9?

God's desire that none should perish but all should come to repentance doesn't change. Man was unwilling to repent even after 120 years of opportunity (see Gen. 6:3). The change is not in God's nature but in man's actions. If God did not judge sin according to His righteous and just standard of holiness, then He wouldn't be immutable. In Noah's case, the people's sin and unwillingness to repent exposed them to God's justice. In Jonah's case, repentance made the Ninevites candidates for God's mercy.

Did God change His will or standards in the story of Nineveh's repentance?

What is God's will and standard according to Romans 2:5-8?

The Ninevites' sin deserved God's wrath; God chose to show them mercy because they showed repentance. God showed mercy according to His righteous and just character.

How would you describe God's response in Noah's story?

How would you describe God's response in Jonah's story?

The answers differed, yet God is the same—immutable. In Noah's story, God regretted and destroyed. In Jonah's story, God relented and showed mercy. Though the outcomes were different, God's standard was the same. If God treated them with different standards, He would have changed. Because He is immutable, God must treat differently those who repent and those who rebel.

Girl, I know this can be a tad confusing. But, remember, our real hope when life doesn't make sense isn't in getting all the right answers and figuring it all out; our real hope is in the encounter we have with God as we explore these mysteries.

Finish up today by reading a psalm of David near the end of his life. Make his prayer in 2 Samuel 22:30-32 your prayer.

Dear God,

Amen

God's way is perfect and His Word is flawless. We must take Him as He is, perfect and flawless. When we can't understand His choices, we trust His character.

Sister, God may have repented He made man, but if you read the Bible cover to cover you will never find Him repenting He redeemed you and me. Now, that's some astounding truth to fill in all your missing pieces! Thank You, Jesus.

A piece of my mind:
God changes His work, but not His will.

Day 4 The God We Don't Expect

We're nearing the end of our study and I don't know about you, but when I look back through what we've considered, it provokes a question. You may have done this study looking for some answers. I hope you found some, but more importantly, I hope you too have a question.

In Psalm 24:10, the psalmist asked the important question I hope you and I echo. It's not very different from the question the disciples asked on the Sea of Galilee.

What did the psalmist ask?

On the Sea of Galilee the disciples asked, "Who then is this? Even the wind and the sea obey Him!" (Mark 4:41). When we truly begin to know this God of mystery and love, we are overwhelmed. We begin to ask: *Who is this God who cares so deeply for us, is always with us, treats us justly, hears our prayers, and is without error? Who is this God who fills in all our missing pieces with Himself?*

Jot down some adjectives that come to mind when you think of God and how you have experienced Him through this study.

Some of my adjectives include: holy, kind, patient, faithful, intimately aware, comforting … my list could go on and on. Yet, though this King of Glory is companionable, He is always to be feared for He is the immutable, holy, complete, perfect God.

Do you think it's possible to love God and fear God at the same time? Why or why not? Read Deuteronomy 6:5 and Isaiah 8:13 to assist you in your answer.

Not only is it possible to fear God and love Him at the same time, we are commanded to. When we grasp the majesty of God and realize we are commanded to fear Him, it can make us wonder *Is He safe? Is He good? If He is so caring, present, and attentive of us, how can we really fear Him if He is good?*

Think about this. Can God be good and still be worthy of our fear? I mean the knee-knocking, fall down in His presence kind of fear? If so, is He really safe? Hmm …

Brace yourself; I'm about to bring up my favorite dead author again. In C.S. Lewis's first book of the Narnia series, the Pevensie children first learn about Aslan. They detect from Mr. and Mrs. Beaver's comments and tone that Aslan must be quite a man. Then they're surprised to find out he is a lion.

> "Ooh!" said Susan, "I'd thought he was a man. Is he—quite safe? I shall feel rather nervous about meeting a lion."

> "That you will, dearie, and no mistake," said Mrs. Beaver, "if there's anyone who can appear before Aslan without their knees knocking, they're either braver than most or else just silly."

> "Then he isn't safe?" said Lucy.

> "Safe?" said Mr. Beaver. "Don't you hear what Mrs. Beaver tells you? Who said anything about safe? 'Course he isn't safe. But he's good. He's the King, I tell you."[6]

Now, if you're not a totally obsessive Lewis-lover like me, you may not be familiar with the Narnia series. So, let me give you the basic gist. C.S. Lewis created the great lion Aslan as a "supposal" of Christ. In other words, suppose there was another world and Christ visited it; Aslan is what He would be like. The point Lewis was making is that the "King of Glory" is good, but He isn't safe. He is worthy of our fear.

What God does command us to do in Leviticus 19:14?

We are told to fear our God because He is the Lord, and we've been told the fear of God doesn't really mean being afraid but, rather, reverent awe. Though fearing God includes reverence, the Hebrew word *yare* used in this verse (and countless others) means *to fear.*[7]

> What do Proverbs 23:17 and Jeremiah 32:38-39 tell us our posture should be before God?

> We should fear God always. Let's see what this looks like. How did God greet Abram in Genesis 15:1?

> How did John react when he was in Christ's presence in Revelation 1:17? What words did Christ speak to him?

Now think with me a moment here. If nothing is to fear in the presence of he Lord—if His mere character evokes no trembling from us—why did God tell these men not to fear? Don't miss the key point. God is a consuming fire; He is holy—both good and fierce.

C.S. Lewis gives us Aslan, who is good and fierce, to provide a balanced depiction of God's character. Some may only perceive God as a harsh judge holding a lightning bolt laser gun just waiting to shoot. Do you see God as only holy and terrible, lacking compassion and love? Or do you cling to an image of a God whose an overgrown, fluffy teddy bear or a cosmic BFF? The complete view of God demands respect and fear.

> How does your own concept of God relate to Lewis's notion of Aslan being both good and fierce, safe but not tame at the same time?

Do you need to adjust your perception of God to better represent who He is? If so, what steps will you take to do so?

Lewis famously wrote that Aslan wasn't safe, but he's good. He's the king. "Who is this King of glory?" the psalmist queried (Ps. 24:8). God is neither safe nor tame, but in every instance His severity is ultimately revealed as love.

Who is this King who cares for us so deeply and fills our missing pieces with real hope? He is the Lion of Judah, the King of kings.

He may be the God we don't expect but He is the God we need.

A piece of truth from David:
"The LORD is great and is highly praised; He is feared above all gods." *Psalm 96:4*

Day 5 Filling in the Missing Peace

Can you believe we are on the last day of this study? I thought of you each time I sat before my computer and wrote. I've asked God to help these lessons make sense to me so I could try to make sense to you. We've grappled with some big questions and I hope the wrestling has made you stronger.

What has been the hardest week of study for you? Why?

What is your most significant "aha" from doing this study?

What challenged you the most in this study?

What quotes or Scriptures do you want to remember?
Write them below.

I've mentioned a few times that our real hope and satisfaction doesn't come from solving mysteries of faith, getting our questions answered, or filling in our missing pieces with some slick Christian sound bite. No, real hope is from the encounter we have with the living God, Yahweh.

Take a few moments to flip through the pages of your book. Notice your reflections, the Scriptures, and your prayers.

What is your most memorable encounter with God over the weeks you've done this study?

Share your answer with a Bible study buddy over coffee or tea. Discussing this with her can help clarify and solidify your thoughts. Be sure to jot down any additional insights you gain from your conversation. The thoughts recorded above can serve as encouragement for you with the missing pieces you may encounter in the future.

We affirmed this week that God is perfect in all His ways; He does not err. That means the missing pieces of your life—challenges you are facing—are part of His perfect plan.

What does Isaiah 45:7 say God does?

So, what does that mean? If God is perfect in all His ways, can disaster and darkness be part of that strange perfection? Think of the missing piece you've dealt with most during this study.

How do you see that your darkness could be part of God's perfect plan?

I've come to the understanding and acceptance that the missing pieces of my life, like blindness and depression, are places God's sovereignty carved out so there would be room for the real hope and peace that sustains me because He does care, He is aware, and He does not err.

Though we may believe God is perfect and caring, there are things we don't understand; there are still mysteries about Him.

Job is someone who can identify with our missing pieces. He had quite a few missing pieces himself.

Summarize what he said about God in Job 36:26; 37:5.

God is exalted, and we do not know Him. He does great things which we cannot comprehend. Sister, when it comes to God, there will always be an element of mystery—things we cannot possibly understand or comprehend.

So, in the midst of the mystery—when you're smack-dab in the middle of a hard missing piece—here are three things I want you to remember.

1. Every missing piece is a snapshot.

What you struggle with—whether it's debt, disease, or any number of difficulties—is not the whole picture. It's just one photo in the whole photo album that is your life. It is not forever. It really will pass away someday. Just like an old photo in an album, the pain will become a faded memory. Keep your missing piece in perspective—eternal perspective. Read 2 Corinthians 4:16-18 when you need to be reminded your missing piece is temporary.

2. Every missing piece is a teacher.

Your struggles may cause you to experience loss, but you can also gain wisdom and deeper understanding as you allow them to teach you. Think about what knowledge you have found in your missing piece. What foolishness have you left behind because of what you learned from it? Read Psalm 25:3; 86:11; Romans 5:3 when you need encouragement in the classroom of suffering.

3. Every missing piece is a ministry.

Your missing pieces can be opportunities to redeem your loss and give to others. For example, the apostle Paul wrote the Books of Colossians, Philemon, Ephesians, and Philippians while he was in prison in Rome. He could have seen that prison—that missing piece— as an opportunity for self-pity or ministry hiatus. Paul could have spent his time in prison asking "Why God?" He could have stared at the shackles he wore and cried out, "God, are You fair? God, are You aware of me in this prison?"

Some people spend their whole lives asking questions of faith like, "God, do You hear prayer? God, are You there? God, do You err?" But, what if you take those same kinds of questions and ask, "Do I care? Am I there for others? Am I aware of the world around me? Am I an answer to the prayers of others?" When we become part of the answer for others who suffer, the questions concerning our own suffering seem to move to a place of less significance.

Consider these questions and ask God how your missing pieces can allow you to minister to others.

How can I show someone else I care?

What can I do to be there for another person?

How can I be a part of God's answer to prayer?

My friend, it can feel like the things of this earth are permanent, but they aren't. They are just a snapshot—a bunch of pieces loosely knit together by our hope, plans, and circumstances. And, even when those pieces are broken or missing, they can still teach us and become a source of ministry. They can actually become a place where we find the missing peace we long for.

First Peter 5:10 reminds us we can have hope when life doesn't make sense. Rewrite this verse as a prayer and replace all the "you's" with "me" and "I."

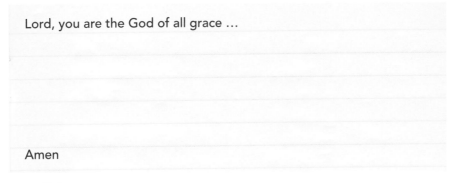

Lord, you are the God of all grace …

Amen

A parting piece of my heart from me to you:
God promises He will fill in all your missing pieces in His time with Himself. Dear Sister, don't settle for less.

1. *Awed to Heaven, Rooted in Earth: Prayers of Walter Brueggemann* (Minneapolis, MN: Augsburg Fortress, 2003), 87.
2. C.S. Lewis, *Mere Christianity* (New York: Touchstone, 1996). Available from the Internet: *www.cslewisinstitute.org*
3. "Kadash," Hebrew for Christians [online, cited 13 April 2012]. Available from the Internet: *www.hebrew4christians. com*
4. "Halig," *The Free Dictionary* [online, cited 13 April 2012]. Available from the Internet: *www.thefreedictionary.com*
5. "Nacham," *NAS Exhaustive Concordance* [onilne, cited 13 April 2012]. Available from the Internet: *www.concordances.org*
6. C.S. Lewis, *The Lion, the Witch, and the Wardrobe* (New York: Macmillan, 1970), 75–76.
7. Brown, Driver, Briggs and Gesenius. "Hebrew Lexicon entry for Yare,'" *The Old Testament Hebrew Lexicon* [online, cited 13 April 2012]. Available from the Internet: *www.studylight.org*

Group Session  7

Video Notes

Psalm 18:30, "His way is _____."

Even when we make _____, God's plan cannot
be _____.

God's plan for you is to _____ in the _____
of what He has already _____.

Blessed is the woman who doesn't quit because she has _____
_____ in her blanket of faith.

Conversation Guide

1. What's the difference between resisting God and resting in Him? How can you
   move from resistance to rest?

2. Without using names, share about a situation in which God turned the mess of
   someone's life into a masterpiece.

3. How will the assurance that God will use the missing pieces of your life as part
   of His perfect plan for you impact your faith journey?

DOWNLOADS

· ·

Video and audio sessions are available
at *lifeway.com/jenniferrothschild*

Jennifer's freebie "15-Day Faith Builder"
available at *JenniferRothschild.com/MP*

WEEKLY APPLICATION APPENDIX

At the end of each week of study, apply the following
actions to help practice and reinforce what you learned.
If you are doing this study without the videos, these are
the applications that conclude each video session.

Session 1: As we begin our study, get a blanket. I call it your blanket of faith. Imagine your blanket has some missing pieces—holes created by the questions that rise from your heartache, trials, or disappointments. Each sorrow creates a hole, a missing piece. As you begin each day in our time together, wrap yourself in that blanket. Feel how it warms and protects you. Your faith does just that for you.

Session 2: For the next five days as you begin your study, begin with prayer. Start with your hands closed to represent what "portion" you may be clinging to. Or perhaps your closed fist should represent anger toward God for what you perceived as His lack of care for you in the past. Then, open your hand to represent letting go of whatever you clung to and let your open hand show a willingness to receive God's compassion for you. Only open hands receive. You cannot receive with a clenched fist. God does care. Let go of whatever is in your hands, open them to God, and receive.

Session 3: For the coming week, take a stack of sticky notes and write the words "thank you" on each one. Place one on anything you are grateful for. Start with ordinary things, "Thank you Lord for this coffee pot; I don't deserve it." (I know you may be thankful for your dog, but, spare Fido the instant hair removal when the note comes off!) Stick a thank-you note on each item. If you become thankful "for" all things, there will be a whole lot of tiny papers around your home! The point is this: when you feel life pinch, when you deal with your missing pieces, take an imaginary sticky note marked with "thank you" and let it fill in your missing piece. Take it from the physical to the spiritual. I hope you go through a whole pad of sticky notes!

Session 4: For the next five days, complete the following two sentences as you begin your Bible study:

Today I _____.

Today God _____.

As you complete your sentences composed of what is true and known, use present tense. The word "if" cannot appear.

Session 5: God does see you. You are in-significant. To help you understand in a tangible way that you are in-significant, that you dwell in the significance of God, write the letter "N" somewhere you will see it all day. Why? Think of it this way: when you buy in to something, when you agree, you say, "I'm in!" Well, you are in … in-significant. So, instead of writing the word I-N, just place a big letter N somewhere you will see it. Perhaps you want to put an "N" in a place where you feel unnoticed. When you see it think, *I'm IN! God is aware of me … I am in-significant!*

Session 6: God does hear your prayer. In fact, He listens for it. Can you entrust yourself into His hands? This week, I want you to "name it and kneel." In other words, name how you have responded in the past to unanswered prayer. Has your response been commitment? Or, have you been angry, hurt, bitter, faithless, or apathetic? Once you name it, pray, "Father, into Your hands I commit my …[name it]" and as you pray, kneel. Kneeling will seal your sense of bowing to God's authority.

Entrust your missing pieces into God's hands.

Session 7: If it's been a while since you threw your blanket of faith over your shoulders, wrap up in it this week. Feel the security, warmth, and protection it brings. As you consider the question, "God, do You err?" think about the missing pieces you have in your blanket of faith and thank God that because He is perfect, you can see His ways more perfectly through each missing piece.

Leader Guide

written by Bethany McShurley

HOSTESS TIPS

Step 1: Advertise a month prior to your first session. Share whether childcare will be provided and if participants pay for their books.

Step 2: Order member books and purchase the group-use video downloads online.

Step 3: Reserve a meeting space and equipment to view the video.

Step 4: Enlist a hospitality assistant to greet, prepare name tags fashioned from cupcake baking wrappers, and plan refreshments. Enlist a prayer assistant who will pray over those in the group both before and during the sessions.

Step 5: Complete your lessons in the member book and view the video portions of the study, including bonus features, prior to group time.

Your job as hostess is to make participants feel welcome, valued, and ready to grasp and apply truths from God's Word. You don't have to serve as a content expert. Instead, model warmth and encourage accountability within the group, facilitate the opening time, pray, show the video, and close the conversation within your time frame. Invite God's Spirit to lead your meetings and don't worry about having the right answer to every question; some are subjective.

Help your group manage their time together by keeping discussion on topic. Should someone dominate, gently insert, "Thanks for sharing. Anyone else?" Affirm participants' comments with a "thank you," even if you disagree with a point. Should a group member begin to talk about odd theology, ask others for input so the Holy Spirit can administer truth through the body of Christ.

Throughout the study, you'll see suggestions to discuss what you're learning with a "Bible study buddy." Encourage your group members to find a friend and talk through the study. This encourages accountability and gives each member a prayer partner.

As you go through the study, note questions for your group to discuss. We have provided suggestions below. We have also designated other questions with a color shadowbox in the text. You know your group best. Follow the Holy Spirit's leading as you determine how you and your group process *Missing Pieces*.

Participants may download freebies for each week at *JenniferRothschild.com/MP*.

SESSION ONE

1. Welcome individuals. Introduce yourself by sharing one item from your purse that reveals something about you. Ask participants to do the same.

2. Distribute member books and introduce Jennifer by briefly sharing her biography (p. 4). Ask for a volunteer to read Jennifer's introduction on pages 5–6.

3. Review the Table of Contents. Encourage participants to share which chapter title question she would most like to ask. Affirm that God understands our concerns and will use this study to deepen our understanding of His love and character. Explain that the text includes learning activities meant to help them apply truths gained. Say: "This week we'll complete pages 8–30."

4. Ask participants to share contact information so that they can serve as Bible study buddies to one another over the coming weeks. Remind participants that you, the hospitality assistant, and the prayer assistant will be praying for them. Encourage them to share with you insights and needs as they arise.

5. Point out the video notes on page 7. Watch session 1 (35:11).

6. Use the conversation guide (p. 7) to begin and stimulate conversation. Do not feel you must complete all questions. Leave two minutes at the end of your discussion to watch Jennifer's closing thoughts.

7. Point out the weekly application index on pages 149–150 for ladies to better remember each weekly challenge. Close in prayer.

SESSION TWO

1. Welcome group members and distribute name tags. Open in prayer, thanking God for His care and loving involvement in the life of each participant.

2. Point out the video notes on page 31. Watch session 2 (27:16).

3. Use the conversation guide, your own notes, and the following questions to lead the group in discussion of the video and the homework.

   • What did God teach you this week about His care for you?

   • Refer participants to page 25. What does Deuteronomy 8:2-3 suggest as the purpose of "being led into the wilderness" or enduring a season of difficulty? How has God revealed His love for you on your journey?

   • How does the following quote on page 27 contrast with your prior ideas regarding God's care? "Delivering us into hard stuff, through hard stuff, and from hard stuff all show God's compassion and care." Read Psalm 66:11-12 for further insight.

   • Have participants describe situations in which they spiritually matured or grew better because of pain (p. 13). (Don't forget to share your story!) Ask how expectation of similar gains might help make future difficulties easier to bear.

   • Ask for a volunteer to read Hebrews 4:15-16. What comfort do you find in knowing that Jesus, our High Priest, can empathize with us in our struggles and hurts? What will we find when we confidently ask God for help (v. 16)?

   • Take turns finishing the sentence, "God, I thank You and praise You for caring so much about _____ that You _____."

4. Return to the video for closing thoughts. Remember the weekly application index also includes each week's challenge.

SESSION THREE

1. Welcome group members by name. Open in prayer, thanking God for His justice, grace, and mercy. Ask Him to increase your faith and to help each participant learn to approach Him with a grateful heart.

2. Point out the video notes on page 53. Watch session 3 (25:45).

3. Use the conversation guide, your own notes, and the following questions to lead the group in discussion of the video and the homework.

- What did God teach you this week about His fairness (justice)?

- Have participants share general issues that might lead some to question God's fairness (for example: famine, disease, suffering). Turn to page 37 and take turns reading aloud the Scriptures listed in the activity. Ask which they choose to memorize and why. Note that God created a world that was "very good" (Gen. 1:31). Humanity's sin ushered in evil, suffering, and death (see Gen. 3:17-18; Rom. 8:22). God will one day set things right (see Rev. 21:3-4).

- Read aloud Romans 6:23 and Psalm 103:10. How does it feel to know that God does not treat us as our sin deserves? Does His mercy support or discredit the notion that God is fair? Explain (p. 43).

- God's grace is free and undeserved favor. It's unmerited kindness (p. 39). On a poster or tear sheet, list as a group the many ways God shows grace to you, His children.

- Enlist a volunteer to read aloud Psalm 73:21-26 where Asaph goes from grumbling over perceived injustice to praising God. How will a grateful response to God over pain change you and lead to the life you desire (p. 47)?

4. Return to the video for closing thoughts. Encourage participants to contact a Bible study buddy at least once while completing their daily assignments. Pray over these partnerships.

SESSION FOUR

· ·

Work with the hospitality assistant to prepare a simple fellowship meal of soup and bread for your group time.

1. Welcome participants and bless the meal. Be certain to thank Jesus that where two or three are gathered in His name, He is in their midst (see Matt. 18:20).

2. Point out the video notes on page 77. Watch session 4 (20:00).

3. Use the conversation guide, your own notes, and the following questions to lead the group in discussion of the video and the homework.

- What did God teach you this week about His presence?

- Turn to page 56. What phrase did you choose to describe your hard place where God seemed absent? Discuss whether those feelings of isolation from God were based on perception or reality. Have a volunteer read aloud Psalm 139:7-12,17-18.

- Share responses to the activity on page 69 about hard places where we experience the presence of God. How might walking in a daily awareness of His presence change the way you approach life? relationships? high points? lows?

- We often base if/then statements on our logic to compensate for the mystery of God's action or inaction (p. 65–66). We need to guard ourselves against filling in missing pieces with our own logic. What if/then statements do you need to get rid of? (If group members are hesitant, begin by sharing your own.)

- Have participants repeat after you, "God is with me ... He always has been ... and He always will be."

4. Don't forget to return to the video for closing thoughts.

SESSION FIVE

1. Read aloud Psalm 139:1-18. Thank God for His intimate knowledge of each life.

2. Point out the video notes on page 101. Watch session 5 (25:11).

3. Use the conversation guide, your own notes, and the following questions to lead the group in discussion of the video and the homework.

- What surprising new detail did God teach you this week about His awareness?

- The Lord is *omniscient*, all-seeing and all-knowing. What specifics did He know about you before you were born (p. 86)? Discuss how it feels to know God already sees remaining chapters of our lives though we are yet to live them.

- Acknowledging God is a God of knowledge is acknowledging that what He knew and knows, He allows and redeems. Why do we sometimes struggle to accept and submit to God's all-knowing character? Enlist a volunteer to briefly share about a tough situation the Lord saw and allowed her to face and then redeemed, bringing remarkable good out of pain.

- Even when we face tragic loss we can find comfort in the truth that God not only knows the actualities, He knows the potentialities (p. 93). How might remaining similarly sensitive to God's unlimited perspective comfort you in the loss of a job, the death of a loved one, or a diagnosis of a chronic problem?

- The Old Testament's use of the word *remember* in connection to God doesn't refer to an "Oh yeah, I forgot!" kind of remembering. What does it mean (p. 99)? Encourage participants to form an explanation of how God, who cannot forget, is able to no longer remember our sins.

4. Return to the video for closing thoughts.

SESSION SIX

1. Open in prayer, thanking God that He hears. Ask Him to be glorified through your group's time together.

2. Point out the video notes on page 125. Watch session 6 (25:15).

3. Use the conversation guide, your own notes, and the following questions to lead the group in discussion of the video and the homework.

- What did God teach you about His attentiveness to the prayers of the righteous, those whose relationship with Him is based on faith in Christ?

- In what two instances does God choose not to hear our prayers? Have a volunteer read Psalm 66:18 and James 4:3 aloud. Discuss the importance of seeking God's will over our own. Share about a time when you sought God's will over yours and, as a result, enjoyed unexpected blessing.

- Share responses to the activities on page 108. How do you typically interpret a person's silence? In what ways might your response to God's silence mirror that tendency? List potential purposes accomplished by God's silences (p. 108–112).

- Describe Habakkuk's stance as he waited on God (see Hab. 2:1). Share and explain posture illustrations from page 116. Discuss practical ways we can show God we are expectantly watchful of His intervention or rescue. What attitudes or actions convey lack of faith in Him?

- Read aloud Habakkuk 3:17-19. Ask how the passage has spoken to group members during the study.

4. Talk through the conversation questions. Then return to the video. Thank participants for their dedication to the study.

SESSION SEVEN

. . . .

Celebrate the study's completion and share a box of assorted chocolates.

1. Open in prayer, praising God that He is righteous and faithful in all His ways. Thank Him for what you've learned through this time of study.

2. Point out the video notes on page 148. Watch session 7 (29:25).

3. Use the conversation guide, your own notes, and the following questions to lead the group in discussion of the video and the homework.

   • What new insight did God give you this week about His righteousness and immutability?

   • Compare and contrast your want ads from pages 129 and 130. Discuss ways to demonstrate to God a desire not to conform Him to your ideas but to be conformed to His image.

   • Imagine a skeptic enters your meeting room and denies the changeless nature of God by citing Genesis 6:5-8 and Jonah 3:10. Working as a group, explain how God's responses to both situations illustrate His immutability.

   • Turn to page 144. Share responses regarding your most significant "aha" moments from recent weeks. What is your most memorable encounter with God's Word over the weeks you've done this study?

   • As we close our time together, how do you need to adjust your perception of God to better represent who He is? What steps will you take to do so?

4. Return to the video for closing thoughts.

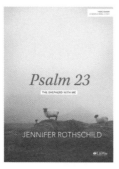